HER TIME

CAROLINE FIELD

A FRONTIER CONVICT

LISA APFEL

ISBN: 978-1-7636376-1-0

Self-published by Lisa Apfel

Cover design by Lisa Apfel

For my family members who agreed to test their DNA.

Without your generosity the links could not be proven.

CONTENTS

ILLUSTRATIONS

Warning to Aboriginal and Torres Strait Islander peoples.

** Members of Aboriginal and Torres Strait Islander communities are respectfully advised that this book contains references to historical violence and includes images of people who have passed away.*

Author's Apology:

To the descendants of the Wiradyuri people who were killed, attacked and forced from their land by my ancestors either directly or indirectly I am sorry. I hope this book goes some way to truth telling. I have done my best to sift through the one-sided colonial accounts and combine them with Wiradyuri information that is available about the events mentioned in this book.

Author's Notes

My notations are in square brackets.

Measurements

This book preserves contemporary units of measurement.

There were twelve pence to a shilling and twenty shillings to a pound.

One acre is equivalent to 0.405 hectares.

A mile is about 1.61 kilometres, and a foot is 30.5 centimetres.

In weight a pound is about 0.45 kilograms.

Symbols

Pre-decimal currency was written in the form:

£	*Pound*
s or /–	*shillings*
d	*pence*

INTRODUCTION

Her Time are a series of books I have written to highlight the amazing women that have come before me. This second book is Caroline Field's story.

Raised in industrial Birmingham, she was a product of poverty. Her peers were the street-fighters and gang members; the early precursors of the peaky blinders. She stood no chance of avoiding the criminal elements of the city and coming under their influence.

The book follows her harrowing journey to Australia and her unique experiences in what was the colony's frontier. It is Wiradyuri country and was past the 'limits of location' beyond which settlers were forbidden to travel. It was a place where only convicts and the military were sent in an effort to grow the food necessary to support the colony. She was vastly outnumbered by men, isolated and away from the law.

Interpreting her actions has been a challenge given the chasm between our modern Australian lives, which are lived in relative comfort and security, and her poor life lived nearly two hundred years ago. Today, we have the benefit of many support services, medical treatments and communication channels, which were unheard of in Caroline's time. Imagine a life without safe painkillers and sanitary products, a life where you couldn't pick up a phone to call your friends and family,

Hers was a time where food was procured locally and often grown at home. Caroline would have hand churned butter and salted meat to try and make it last more than a couple of days. She would have sewn her own clothes by hand and then hand washed them in hot water that been heated over an open fire. She would have waited months before making the long walk to town for essentials like candles or fabrics. Most bush homes in the frontier were nothing but rudimentary huts with dirt floors and bark walls that offered little insulation from either the bitter winters or the sweltering summers. They contained a fireplace over which all the cooking was done and around which families gathered. That was Caroline's world and through that lens we get an appreciation of her struggles and her resilience.

Archives have been scoured in England and Australia to track and reconstruct Caroline's life. Records mentioning her proved to be very scarce and DNA evidence was used to confirm her origins and her children.

The people in her life and the facts surrounding them have been extensively researched and are integral to telling Caroline's story. Their individual stories are expanded on in the epilogue.

Caroline's life, although full of struggles, was nothing but a pure success story. She had eight children that can be identified through the records and through the DNA analysis. Those children and their children have gone on multiplying.

I hope you enjoy reading about Caroline and I hope her story will now live on without fading away into history.

CHAPTER 1
INDUSTRIAL MELTING POT

In the year 1815, near the geographic centre of England, lies the city of Birmingham. A city experiencing rapid growth thanks to the industrial revolution. It stood as a world leader in metal works, manufacturing a vast array of products, including guns, jewellery, swords, files, toys and brass. A substantial proportion of the workers were artisans producing high quality bespoke products in small workshops within their houses, which was a stark contrast to the large factories dominating London and Manchester. These specialised operations gave workers the flexibility to quickly adapt and redesign their products as the market demanded, resulting in premium quality and allowing them to charge premium prices; A necessity given the extra travel costs associated with Birmingham's inland location.[1]

On the 26th of October,[2] a young unmarried woman named Sarah Field gave birth to her daughter, Caroline. Sarah lived in Wood Street near the burial grounds. It was a 'black spot' on the face of the city,"[3] where gangs of thieves were birthed.

The burial grounds had opened eight years before Caroline's birth because the churchyard of St Martin-in-the-Bullring was overwhelmed by the increased population.

> *Poor health was widespread at the time; poverty, hunger and overcrowding were everywhere. People were dying from diseases linked with heavy pollution, a lack of adequate healthcare and malnutrition as well as conditions and accidents associated with dangerous work practices.*[4]

When baby Caroline was six months old, Sarah arranged her baptism at St. Phillip's Cathedral in the heart of the city, officially giving her, her surname, Field.

After three years of raising Caroline alone, Sarah married her neighbour William Horton,[5] who worked as a japanner.[6] Japanning was a finishing and decorating technique applied to wood, leather, tin, and papier-mâché. It created a shiny black surface that was then hand painted with flowers or other decorative images to imitate the highly decorative lacquered items coming from Japan.

Sarah and William welcomed a son named Joseph on the 5th of November 1819, followed by Samuel two years later. The two boys remained unbaptised until the

---

[1] Nuttall, Bryan. 2014. 'Birmingham's Manufacturing History'. *RH Nuttall* (blog). 11 February 2014. https://www.rhnuttall.co.uk/blog/birminghams-manufacturing-history/.

[2] 'Birmingham, England, Church of England Baptisms, 1813-1922 for Caroline Field, Birmingham, St Phillip, 1813-1818'. n.d. Ancestry. Accessed 29 March 2022. Image 301. https://www.ancestry.com.au.

[3] 'Park Street Burial Ground and Birmingham's Population Expansion.' 2016. *MOLA Headland Infrastructure* (blog). Accessed 1 June 2024. https://molaheadland.com/park-street-burial-ground-and-birminghams-population-expansion/.

[4] Ibid.

[5] 'Birmingham, England, Church of England Marriages and Banns, 1754-1937 for Sarah Field, Aston, St Peter and St Paul, 1817-1820'. n.d. Ancestry. Accessed 29 March 2022. Image 95. https://www.ancestry.com.au.

[6] 'Warwickshire Baptisms. St Martin in Birmingham for Joseph and Samuel Horton. Baptised 2 Sep 1822'. Findmypast. Accessed 31 March 2022. https://www.findmypast.com.au/

following September, when the ceremony was conducted at St Martin's.[7] A year later saw the birth of another son, John.[8]

William would have set up a home-based workshop, in their Wood Street home, being paid on a piece rate basis, where the more he produced the more he was paid. In order to produce as many pieces as possible all family members, even young children like Caroline, had to help out. It was a tough upbringing with all her spare time spent in production and no time to play.

The popularity of japanned products started to wane in the 1820's, and the income of the young family would have deteriorated. William had to find work elsewhere and was working as a glazier by 1828. The transition to a new career for William would have required time and training, and likely left the family in need of support.

The only support for families who fell on tough times was provided by the Birmingham Asylum for the Infant Poor. This institution admitted pauper children aged five years and older and put them to work in manufacturing industries. In 1822 they started providing some basic reading education. Whilst no records of admissions survive, we know Caroline could read[9] and it seems plausible that this is where she would have learned. In 1826 when Caroline was eleven there were 389 children in the asylum. They were employed in tasks such as bead-stringing, glass-cutting and the manufacture of small wire items.[10]

In 1828 the family continued growing with the birth of a fourth boy, Alfred. When little Alfred was four months old, Sarah and William took him and five-year-old John, to St Martin's to be baptised.[11]

Gang violence continued around Birmingham with the newspapers reporting that "the frequency of midnight depredations…renders it necessary for all persons to be upon their guard."[12] The area around their Wood Street home was a particular area of concern.[13]Caroline had been growing up surrounded by these influences and many of the young offenders were her peers.

Work was almost impossible to find so William diversified his sources of income by venturing into plumbing work. The change in work coincided with a change of address and the family moved closer to the city centre, to Lionel Street. It was here that Sarah gave birth to a daughter, Harriet in 1830.[14]

---

[7] Ibid.

[8] 'Warwickshire Baptisms. St Martin's, Birmingham for John and Alfred Horton. Baptised 1 Sep 1828' . Findmypast. Accessed 31 March 2022. www.findmypast.com.au.

[9] Wiblin, Sue. 2019. 'Female Convicts at Bathurst, 1820-1840: A Preliminary Study of Demography, Management and Marriage in Colonial New South Wales'. *Journal of Australian Colonial History* 21: 56. https://search-informit-org.ezproxy.slv.vic.gov.au/doi/10.3316/ielapa.856321164464022.

[10] Nejedly, Mary. July 2018. 'Child Labour in an Industrial Town: A Study of Child Workers in Birmingham, 1750 to 1880'. UBira E Theses. University of Birmingham. Accessed 29 March 2022. https://etheses.bham.ac.uk/id/eprint/9026/1/Nejedly2019PhD.pdf.

[11] 'Warwickshire Baptisms. St Martin's, Birmingham for John and Alfred Horton. Baptised 1 Sep 1828' . Findmypast. Accessed 31 March 2022. www.findmypast.com.au.

[12] *Birmingham Gazette*. 2 Nov 1829. 'BIRMINGHAM, Nov. 2, 1829'. British Library Newspapers. Accessed 3 June 2024. 3. https://link-gale-com.rp.nla.gov.au/apps/doc/EN3216064618/BNCN?sid=bookmark-BNCN&xid=b536ddfe.

[13] *Leamington Spa Courier*. 7 Feb 1829. 'Warwick.' British Library Newspapers. Accessed 3 June 2024. 3. https://link-gale-com.rp.nla.gov.au/apps/doc/JA3230983899/BNCN?sid=bookmark-BNCN&xid=81bd9cf1.

[14] 'Warwickshire Baptisms. St Martin's, Birmingham for Harriet Horton. Baptised 27 May 1831'. Findmypast. Accessed 31 March 2022. www.findmypast.com.au.

The financial pressures meant that fifteen-year-old Caroline was expected to contribute to the family income. She had no experience and finding work was a challenging prospect. The work was labour-intensive and poorly paid making it impossible for a young girl to earn a living wage. Her ability to get a decent job was compounded by her appearance. No matter how much grooming she did, her worn and patched old clothes were like a neon sign highlighting her poverty.

Caroline's friend Sarah Workman was in the same predicament, so they decided to try and improve their chances by stealing some clothes. On the 11th of November 1830 they stole two dresses, two petticoats, one apron, one pinafore, two shawls, two pairs of shoes and a shirt and handkerchief.[15]

The two girls remained undetected for two weeks, when magistrate I Spooner esq. issued indictments for their arrest. The details of the hearings have not been found but it seems likely that the two owners of the clothing, John Kingswood and Daniel Gutteridge, would have made statements identifying the stolen clothes.

Caroline was arrested under the alias of Caroline Hinchley.[16] No details as to why she chose that name or for how long she had been using it have been found. Even though it was her first offence, the use of an alias implies she was trying to protect her name. She knew that if arrested more than once she would be sentenced to transportation. It was not the action of a novice.

Once she was arrested, Caroline was taken and kept in the town gaol. Located in Moor Street, back near their old Wood Street home. The gaol consisted of a sunken courtyard known as "The Hole" surrounded by eight-metre-high walls. There were sixteen cells in two rows, one level with The Hole and the other at street level. They measured just 6ft by 8ft and were likened to dog kennels, being windowless, filthy and exposed to the open air.[17] Inside was an iron bed fitted with manacles ready to shackle a prisoner if needed. Caroline's "allowance was a pennyworth [150 g] of bread and a slice of cheese twice a day, and the use of the pump,"[18] for any water she needed.

Sometime over the next forty days she was transferred to the county gaol cell in Warwick thirty kilometres away where she was to stand trial at the Quarter Sessions. The trip was made in the prison caravan with up to a dozen other prisoners. She and Sarah were shackled until their arrival when they were handed over to the jailer. The jailer placed them in a holding cell and then processed them one by one.

[15] 'Caroline Hinchley alias Field in Depositions, 1824-1850 in the Warwickshire Quarter Sessions. Film #004414588. Images 255-256'. 1831. FamilySearch. Accessed 2 June 2024. www.familysearch.org.

[16] Ibid.

[17] Hutton, William. 1836. *An History of Birmingham*. 6th ed. Birmingham, England: James Guest. Accessed 13 May 2024. 406-407. http://archive.org/details/historybirmingh00huttgoog.

[18] Harman, Thomas T. 1885. 'Showell's Dictionary of Birmingham.' Project Gutenberg. Accessed 09 April 2024. https://www.gutenberg.org/ebooks/14472

Figure 1: The Caravan[19]

THE CARAVAN.

Caroline was taken from the holding cell and strip searched. Her belongings were taken, her clothes were sent for fumigation and her linen was taken to be marked with her initials. She was made to bathe and was given prison clothes made of a course drab woollen cloth. She was allocated a wooden spoon and wooden quart pot for eating and drinking from. Leaving the bathroom she walked through the prison, passing the stone paved exercise yard and dining hall with its long table and fireplace, to her shared cell. Before entering she was made to take off her shoes. With the door closed behind her she would have walked barefoot across the cold brick floor to her iron framed bed. Sitting on the straw mattress two or three cellmates would have watched her.

Her meagre weekly food allowance was strictly controlled. Every morning at 9am she lined up for her daily loaf of bread. It was small and weighed about 500g. This was all she got to eat on Wednesdays and Saturdays. On Mondays and Thursdays, she also got a piece of meat weighing about 250g and on Tuesdays and Fridays she was given 500g of potato. On Sundays, her quart pot was filled with a basic porridge made by cooking oats in water. It was known as gruel.

It was the middle of winter and not where she would have wished to spend Christmas.

On the 4th of January 1831, Caroline was escorted on the walk from her cell to the court room of the shire hall. Her case was presided over by a Justice of the Peace

[19] Hacker, Edward H. n.d. *The New Sporting Magazine Vol 14 January 1838. No. 81*. Google. Accessed 4 April 2024. 428 https://play.google.com/store/books/details?id=wvM7AAAAIAAJ.

who was permitted to try non-capital crimes such as hers. It was a first offence, and she was sentenced "to be imprisoned and kept at hard labour in the House of Correction."[20] Sarah received the same sentence.[21]

The House of Correction also known as the Bridewell was across the road from the gaol.[22] The women sentenced to hard labour were put to work in the kitchen where fires had to be fed and pots scoured.

Caroline's three months were completed on the 25th of March, and she returned to Birmingham where she was caught stealing again, four months later. Her reasons are not recorded which leaves us to ponder why. Was she was forced through desperation or was it a choice.

This time round she chose smaller items that could be secreted away and sold off more easily. She stole a bible, a spelling book, a bed shawl, a blue pocket handkerchief, a piece of blue cotton print fabric and a pair of boys shoes, from the house of watchmaker, James Russell.[23]

She had gotten up early on Tuesday the 5th of July and made her way to Smallbrook Street. All was quiet at number one, James Russell's house, so she opened the door. Taking stock of what items were in reach she stuffed her chosen loot into the pocket of her apron and exited, leaving the door ajar. She made a beeline for Aston where she presumably knew that she could sell the items.

Travelling the backroads and alleys from Smallbrook Street on one side of the city to Lawley Street on the other took her an hour and a half. As she made her way along Lawley Street constable William Hart approached her. She must have raised his suspicion because he stopped and searched her. He later said,

> *I stopped her and examined the things and I found the Bible, Spelling Book, Shoes, Shawl, Handkerchief and Cotton print...I asked her where she got them and she said she brought them from her Mothers and they belonged to her Aunt Field.*[24]

He took the items and her details and let her go. Towards the end of the month James Russell's wife, Elizabeth, identified the items as hers. The case was raised with the magistrate I Spooner, who heard the depositions of both Elizabeth and constable Hart and issued an arrest warrant for Caroline.[25]

Caroline was arrested and taken to the town gaol. Entering and seeing the dog kennel cells and The Hole would have been like entering a recurring nightmare. She soon learned that her case was allocated to the Quarter Sessions, meaning another shackled trip back to Warwick.

---

[20] Caroline Hinchley alias Field in Depositions. Familysearch.

[21] 'Caroline Hinchley in Calendars of Prisoners, 1801-1850, in the Warwickshire Quarter Sessions Film #4415779. Image 340'. 1831. FamilySearch. Accessed 2 June 2024. www.familysearch.org

[22] Smith, William (Topographer). 1830. *A New & Compendious History, of the County of Warwick*. Birmingham, W. Emans. Accessed 2 June 2024. 31. http://archive.org/details/newcompendioushi01smit.

[23] *Birmingham Journal. 1831. 'Warwickshire Quarter Sessions', 22 October 1831. 3. https://www.britishnewspaperarchive.co.uk/viewer/BL/0000224/18311022/039/0003?browse=true.*

[24] 'The King v Caroline Field in Depositions, 1824-1850 in the Warwickshire Quarter Sessions. Film #004414588. Images 37-40'. 1831. FamilySearch. Accessed 2 June 2024. https://www.familysearch.org/search/catalog/show?availability=Family%20History%20Library.

[25] 'Caroline Field in Calendars of Prisoners, Michaelmas Quarter Session Case 38. Ref. QS 26/2/219'. 1831. Warwickshire Records Office.

Stepping out of the prison van at the county gaol, her knowledge of the looming strip search must have filled her with dread. She was taken and put in her cell which was "unfit for purpose, suffering from poor conditions and overcrowding."[26]Here she waited for her trial.

On the 18th of October, Caroline fronted the court. The scene was familiar and so were some of the faces. The turnkey of the the county gaol, William Townson confirmed that she had previously been "convicted of felony,"[27] the clerk was the same face she had seen last time recording the proceedings and she recognised constable Hart. The case against her was proven and because it was a repeat offence she was sentenced to seven years transportation.

Leaving the court, she was taken back to her cell, The solid timber door had one small, barred opening at the top. This was her only view of the dim world beyond. Autumn had begun and it was getting colder by the day. All through winter and spring she sat in that cell until she was taken down to London with the other Warwickshire women bound for New South Wales.

Figure 2: Warwick Gaol Cell Door[28]

[26] 'Warwick Prison, Cape Road.' n.d. *Our Warwickshire* (blog). Accessed 1 April 2022. https://www.ourwarwickshire.org.uk/content/article/warwick-prison-cape-road.

[27]'England & Wales, Criminal Registers, 1791-1892 for Caroline Field. England. Warwickshire. 1831'. 2009. Ancestry. 2009. Image 33. https://www.ancestry.com.au/.

[28] The Carlisle Kid. n.d. 'Former Cell Door - Barrack Street, Warwick-April 2019'. Geograph. Accessed 9 April 2024. https://www.geograph.org.uk/photo/6117556.

CHAPTER 2
OUTBREAK TO OUTPOST

The women boarded the Fanny convict ship at Blackwall on the 23rd of June 1832. It was a wooden barque of 275 tons[29].

Figure 3: Wooden Barque *Royal Tar* 598 tons at Port Adelaide[30]

On the 3rd of July as the *Fanny* made its way down the Thames to Sheerness, with 106 female prisoners.[31]The ship's surgeon, Francis Logan was informed that a sailor was sick. His diagnosis was easy because London was in the midst of a cholera outbreak. Logan sent a messenger to report the case to the authorities and the ship was stopped at Little Nore, near Sheerness and quarantined. In quarantine Logan was bought case after case, the inevitable result of having a contagious disease in a confined space. He administered treatments on eighty-three cases and pronounced death on six.

Due to the high caseload an Assistant Surgeon was seconded to join the *Fanny*. His name was William Marshall of the Royal Navy[32].

Cholera is caused by infection of the intestine with Vibrio cholerae bacteria, leading to severe diarrhoea and subsequent dehydration, which in turn can lead to shock, coma, and death within hours. Transmission occurs when a person ingests

[29] *Sydney Herald.* 1833. 'Shipping Intelligence. Arrivals,' 4 February 1833. National Library of Australia. 2. http://nla.gov.au/nla.news-article12846196.

[30] '"Royal Tar" Wooden Barque at Port Adelaide.' n.d. State Library of South Australia. Accessed 3 April 2022. https://collections.slsa.sa.gov.au/resource/PRG+1373/42/14.

[31] 'Transportation Register of Convicts Bound for New South Wales on the Convict Ship Fanny. Caroline Field HO 11/8/370'. 1832. The National Archives, Kew.

[32] Sydney Herald. 1833.

food or water contaminated with infected faecal matter. Hygiene standards on board were rudimentary, and the bacteria were on every surface.

Medical understanding of how diseases like cholera were caused was in its infancy. The Central Board of Health in London recommended that clothing, bedding, personal effects "and sleeping places of all persons on board vessels from infected ports, ought to be opened, aired, and purified, during three days after arrival."[33]It was known that germs spread, but exactly what they were and how they spread was unknown. The discovery that cholera was contracted by ingesting contaminated food or water had not yet been made, so rather than having effective cleaning and hygiene regimes that would break the chain of transmission, doctors persisted in offering treatments that aimed to mitigate the symptoms. Bloodletting was done to relieve headaches and opium was given to stop spasms.[34] It was hit and miss whether a patient lived or died. Francis Logan utilized these and various other treatments, including calomel (mercury), sinapism (a poultice primarily made of powdered mustard), carbonate of ammonia, magnesia, heat application and rubbing camphorated spirit. Unfortunately, he was unaware that bloodletting worsened dehydration and that the use of mercury posed toxic risks. On a brighter note, the opium he administered proved mercifully effective in pain management, albeit with a considerable risk of addiction.

Caroline did not escape the outbreak and was diagnosed with cholera two days after the first case. The ship's list of sick patients simply notes that the nineteen-year-old was "cured" nine days later. It records that she continued suffering from diarrhoea, for a further nine days, a clear sign she was still ill.[35] Francis Logan dutifully recorded the treatments that he gave to the cholera patients, however no detailed notes on Caroline's treatment were recorded because Francis Logan had also contracted the disease. Assistant surgeon Marshall took over patient care, but he did not record any treatments. Even though the specifics of her treatment weren't detailed we can assume they mirrored those that were.

The first most detailed case Logan recorded was that of Jane Harrison. For seven days she had:

> *cholera spasms with great pain, vomiting and purging. Skin cold and of a leaden hue. Pulse scarcely felt at the wrist...Complained of violent headache vomiting and spasms again very severe with constant purging...During the night she had frequent attacks of vomiting and purging with spasms...Purging and pain in the bowels still severe, pulse 100 skin hot, tongue white has less thirst...Purging still very troublesome...Was taken very ill during the night with cold shivering violent pains spasms purging and vomiting...From this*

---

[33] Central Board of Health. n.d. *The Cholera Gazette: Consisting of Documents Communicated by the Central Board of Health, with Intelligence Related to the Disease, Derived from Other Authentic Sources Jan 14, 1832.* 2nd ed. Vol. 1. London: S. Highley. Accessed 2 April 2022. 7.
https://play.google.com/store/books/details?id=0_EEAAAAQAAJ&rdid=book-0_EEAAAAQAAJ&rdot=1.

[34] Logan, Francis. n.d. 'UK, Royal Navy Medical Journals, 1817-1856. Fanny. 02 Jun 1832-19 Feb 1833'. Ancestry. Accessed 2 April 2022. https://www.ancestry.com.au.

[35] Ibid, Image 27.

attack she did not recover til (sic) in the dawn having almost daily a cold shivering fever and purging.[36]

The ship set sail on the 29th of July in the peak of summer. cholera continued spreading on board for a further month.

The *Fanny* sailed over the equator, a fortnight later at which point the women started coming down with fevers and scurvy. Caroline was recorded on the sick list suffering from a fever and was sick for a week. Logan said that the women who got scurvy, were those "who had been most exhausted by sickness."[37]

The ship reached the Cape of Good Hope, at the southern tip of Africa, in mid-October. Dropping anchor in Simons Bay where Logan arranged for vegetables to be bought on board, and all the "scorbutic patients recovered like magic."[38]A week later no one was on the sick list. They remained at anchor for seven weeks where all the woman except one, Fanny Barr, "got stout or even fat."[39]Hard to believe given how sick they had all been. After leaving the Cape it wasn't long before the sick list grew with forty-nine cases of fever. The surgeon attributed it to "the effects of the cold damp atmosphere."[40]

Caroline along with the other ninety surviving women and nine children arrived in Sydney Harbour on the 1st of February 1833.[41] The journey to Sydney had taken almost seven months.

The women were made to remain on board whilst arrangements were made.[42] Seeing the settlement within reach and being made to stay on board must have been frustrating. All the women and crew would have longed for solid ground and fresh air after their disease riddled journey.

While they waited, the Colonial Secretary came on board to inspect and muster the women in the presence of the surgeon, the captain and the crew. He needed to plan for their dispersal on disembarkation. Notices were run in the local paper informing families who wanted female servants, that they could apply before the 14th to have a prisoner from the recently arrived *Fanny* assigned to them. They were required to enter into a contract to keep them for a month or be fined forty shillings.[43]

After two weeks the women were given the order to leave the ship, where their legs would have "felt very fatigued…in consequence of being so long confined on board a ship."[44]They were taken to the Female Factory, where all female convicts were distributed to their various work assignments. Caroline found out she was

---

[36] Ibid, Images 2-4.

[37] Ibid, Image 34.

[38] Ibid, Image 21.

[39] Ibid.

[40] Ibid, Image 34.

[41] Sydney Herald. 1833.

[42] *Currency Lad*. 1833. 'Shipping Intelligence', 16 February 1833. National Library of Australia. 2. http://nla.gov.au/nla.news-article252637059.

[43]*New South Wales Government Gazette*. 1833. 'Government Gazette Notices', 6 February 1833. National Library of Australia. 51. http://nla.gov.au/nla.news-article230389720.

[44] 'The Wellington Valley Project. Letters and Journals Relating to the Church Missionary Society Mission to Wellington Valley, NSW, 1830-45. A Critical Electronic Edition.' 2002. The University of Newcastle, Australia. 2002. Porter's Journal. https://downloads.newcastle.edu.au/library/cultural%20collections/the-wellington-valley-project/.

going to Bathurst,[45]a place she had never heard of, but soon discovered was very remote.

She and fourteen other women from the *Fanny* were "dispatched in that ponderous machine, 'The Factory Van,' drawn by six horses."[46] The poor animals had a tough time pulling the immense weight of the van, a task that would have been much better suited to a bullock team. No images or further descriptions of the factory caravan have been found. It was a larger more cumbersome precursor to the Black Maria van shown below. Likely having tall wheels to traverse river crossings[47] but with a steel spring suspension that offered little to no cushioning. Caroline would have been jolted around violently as the van drove over ruts and bumps.[48]

Figure 4: Horse Drawn Prison Van or Black Maria[49]

[45] 'New South Wales, Australia, Settler and Convict Lists, 1787-1834. Convicts Arrived 1833-1834. Image 253'. n.d. Ancestry. Accessed 3 April 2022. https://www.ancestry.com.au.

[46] *Currency Lad.* 1833. 'BATHURST.', 16 March 1833. National Library of Australia. 3. http://nla.gov.au/nla.news-article252636401.

[47] Grant, Andrew. 2010. 'Powerhouse Collection - Reading Type Horse-Drawn Caravan'. Powerhouse Collection. 2010. https://collection.powerhouse.com.au/object/408922.

[48] 'Nowland's Mail Coach.' n.d. National Museum of Australia. Accessed 13 August 2023. https://www.nma.gov.au/explore/collection/highlights/nowlands-mail-coach.

[49] *Horse Drawn Prison van or 'Black Maria.'* 1907. Queensland Police Museum. https://ehive.com/collections/3606/objects/553902/horse-drawn-prison-van-or-black-maria.

Figure 5: Sketch of the Roads to Bathurst 1830.[50]

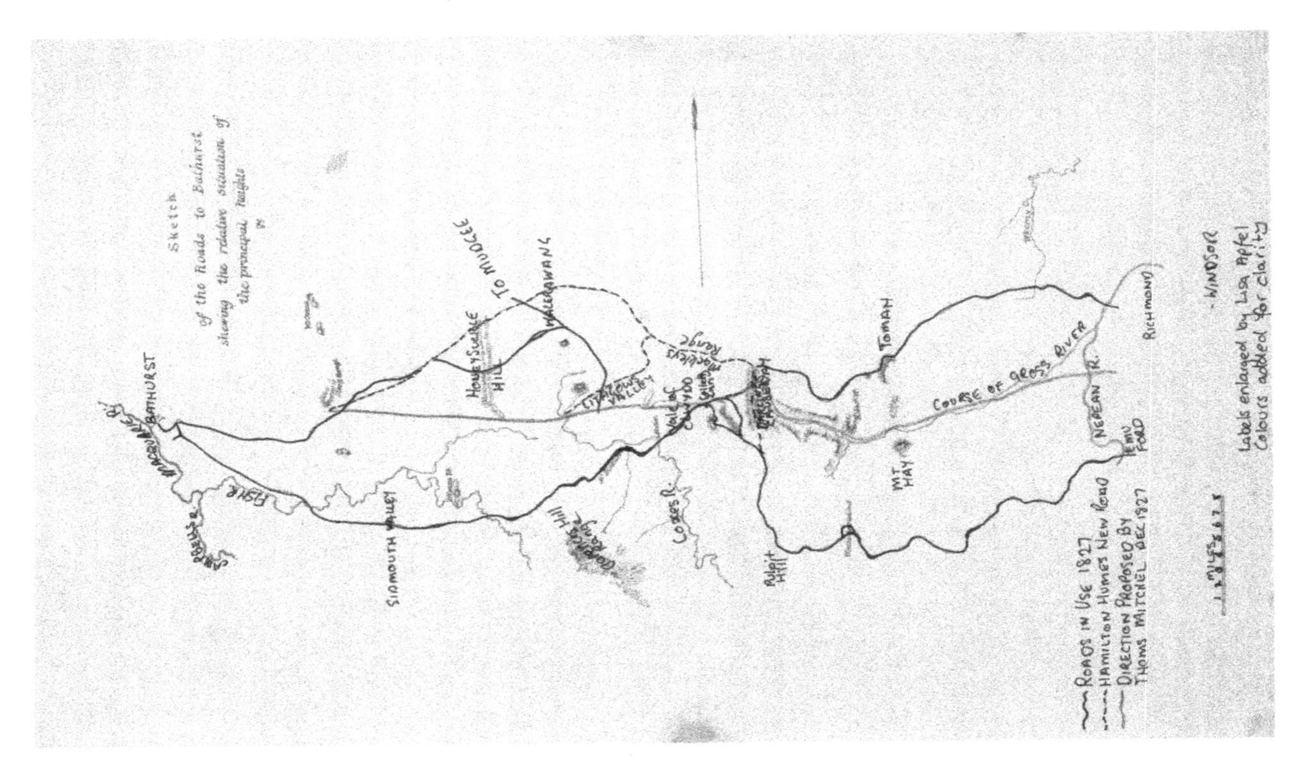

[50] Mitchell, Thomas. 1830. Opp. P8 Sketch of Roads to Bathurst in: Illustrations from Progress in Public Works & Roads in NSW, 1827-1855. Image 7. State Library of New South Wales. Accessed 6 April 2022. https://collection.sl.nsw.gov.au/record/92eVDzPY/265w7QO20MEX0r.

Her trip to Bathurst took fourteen days,[51] which was a pretty standard journey time. The mail run was much quicker, only taking three days,[52] but in poor weather conditions and with heavy loads some parties took up to thirty days to arrive.

Six months before Caroline made the trip, the Reverends Handt and Watson had embarked on their journey. After camping at the foot of the Blue Mountains it took a full day to climb to the top. The steep climb having to be done twice with "the carrier's oxen and those of our own dray were yoked together to take up first his dray and then ours."[53]

During the two days spent crossing the mountains, they encountered "a party of 16 or 18 of the Iron Gang (men who work on the roads in irons) ...escorted by a detachment of the Military." They also learned that the "post-man had been robbed of the mail and most of his clothes, on his way from Bathurst to Sydney.[54]

When Spot, their horse, refused to pull the cart, a passing dray carrying two female convicts offered the reverends' wives a lift. The convict women's "loose and abusive conversation more than overbalanced the advantage which Mrs. W and Mrs. Handt derived from not having to walk."[55]

Figure 6: Chain Gang ca. 1831[56]

Descending the Blue Mountains at Victoria Pass was particularly treacherous, requiring them to fell trees to secure the dray and control its speed of descent.

[51] Wiblin, Sue. 2019. 'Female Convicts at Bathurst, 1820-1840: A Preliminary Study of Demography, Management and Marriage in Colonial New South Wales'. *Journal of Australian Colonial History* 21: 41. https://search-informit-org.ezproxy.slv.vic.gov.au/doi/10.3316/ielapa.856321164464022.

[52] 'The Wellington Valley Project.' Porter's Journal.

[53] 'The Wellington Valley Project,' Handt's Journal.

[54] 'The Wellington Valley Project,' Watson's Journal.

[55] Ibid.

[56] Bruce, G. 1831. *Hobart Town Chain Gang*. State Library of New South Wales. https://collection.sl.nsw.gov.au/digital/R5mDqlVXvZVdq.

Figure 7: Victoria Pass 1830-1835[57]

Over the next couple of weeks, they interacted with other travellers, a road gang, and Aboriginal people, offering prayers and engaging in conversations with each group. Local farmer, William Lane,[58] offered some local hospitality when the group's bullocks strayed one night. The wives stayed in his house near present day Tarana with his family whilst flour and cake was provided to the men, who were searching for the strays. After two days, they continued and completed their arduous thirty-day journey to Bathurst.

Caroline's journey in February was vastly different from that of the reverends in August. Her trip was in summer, and the region was experiencing drought conditions,[59] with flies and mosquitoes becoming constant nuisances. The scorching heat and dry conditions would have made sleeping uncomfortable, a wholly new experience for Caroline.

The convict women were accompanied by the "new matron [of the new Bathurst Female Factory], one constable and a mounted policeman,"[60]responsible for controlling and protecting them. Approaching Cox's River, near the convict stockade, the horses refused to pull the weight of the factory van any further and

[57] Govett, William Romaine. n.d. 'Incident on the Road at Victoria Pass between Pp 6-7 of William Govett Notes and Sketches Taken during a Surveying Expedition in N. South Wales and Blue Mountains Road by William Govett on Staff of Major Mitchell, Surveyor General of New South Wales, 1830-1835.' State Library of New South Wales. Accessed 6 April 2022. https://collection.sl.nsw.gov.au/record/9NaApV5Y/qzANlroa2WqL.

[58] Authors note: William Lane is my 4x great grandfather through a different family branch. He arrived in 1823 as a free settler.

[59] *Sydney Gazette and New South Wales Advertiser*. 1833. 'Agricultural Report for February 1833. Nepean,' 7 March 1833. National Library of Australia. 3. http://nla.gov.au/nla.news-article2211045.

[60] Wiblin. 41.

Caroline and the other "frail ones" had to walk the rest of the way. They managed to travel about eight to ten miles a day.[61]

Figure 8: Convict Stockade at Cox's River Crossing[62]

Caroline's emotions would have shifted between relief and fear. Breathing fresh air, consuming fresh food and water were simple joys she must have appreciated after the choleric conditions of the ship, but then fear of what may lie ahead. Who would she meet, how would she be treated, where was she going, would she suffer depredations or have plenty, and what would she have to do to survive?

On day fourteen the women reached Bathurst, located on the traditional lands of the Wiradyuri nation. It was a government outpost located on the western side of the Macquarie River, used solely for raising the government animal herds. Private individuals were not allowed to live west of the river,[63] but that was about to change. Thomas Mitchell the Surveyor General had recently received instructions from Governor Bourke to draw up a plan for the township.

---

[61] *Currency Lad.* 1833. 'BATHURST.'

[62] *[Convict Stockade at Cox's River Crossing near Hartley]*. 1831. Mitchell Library, State Library of New South Wales. Accessed 10 May 2024. https://collection.sl.nsw.gov.au/record/1l417a51/yxZLXBmdPKMJz.

[63] Hendy-Pooley, Grace. 1905. 'Early History of Bathurst and Surroundings'. *Journal and Proceedings The Australian Historical Society*, 28 November 1905. https://www.rahs.org.au/wp-content/uploads/2015/05/08_Reflecting_Early-History-of-Bathurst-and-Surroundings.pdf.

Figure 9: 1833 Plan for the Town of Bathurst[64]

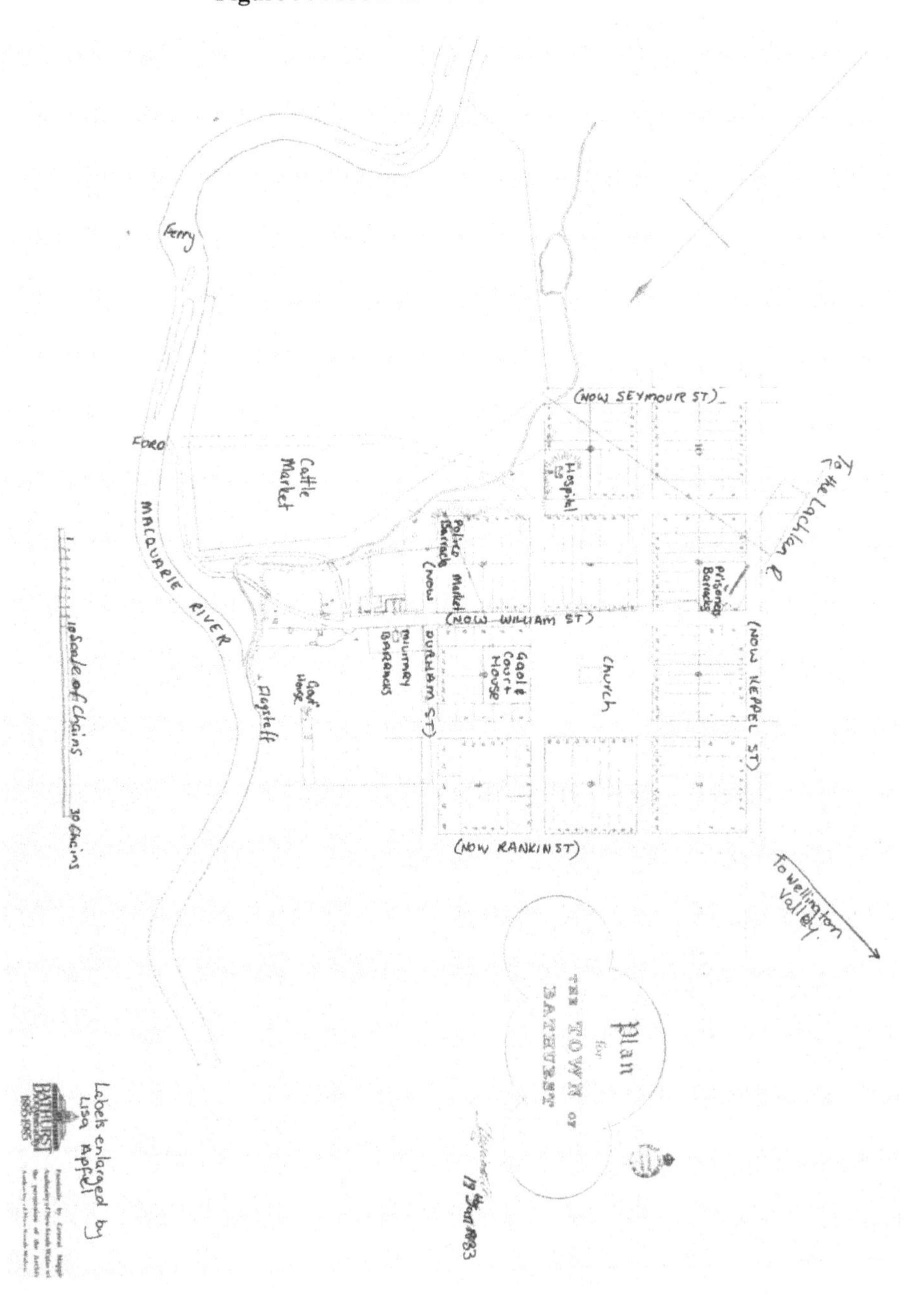

---

[64] Mitchell, Thomas. 1833. *Plan for the Town of Bathurst.* National Library of Australia. Accessed 6 April 2022. http://nla.gov.au/nla.obj-1494744991.

The white population who were permitted to be west side of the river were scattered throughout the region and were engaged primarily in looking after stock. There were about two thousand of them and most were convicts.[65] The women only numbered about fifty.[66]

Caroline arrived at the outpost and was sent straight to the new Female Factory located in the old prisoner's barracks. It "consisted of one large room for the inmates and a separate ground-floor room for the matron."[67] It was missing a privy "which decency ...cleanliness and health imperiously demand."[68]

After evaluating the skills of each woman against the needs of settlers[69] they were "immediately assigned to the most respectable applicants."[70]Caroline, was listed as a "housemaid, all work"[71]and found herself assigned to the matron. Mrs. Black, who was only twenty-seven-years-old.[72] She had gotten to know all the girls on the trip and she chose Caroline.

Figure 10: Bathurst, c.1847-57[73]

[65]'Historical Australian Towns: Bathurst, NSW: Australia's First Inland Settlement.' n.d. *Historical Australian Towns* (blog). Accessed 5 April 2022. https://historicalaustraliantowns.blogspot.com/2018/02/bathurst-australias-first-inland.html.

[66] Wiblin. 28.

[67] Wiblin. 39.

[68] Ibid.

[69] Wiblin. 37.

[70] 'Main Series of Letters Received,1826-1982. [4-2201-2] 33_2396. Evernden to Colonial Secretary.' 1833, 1833. Museums of History NSW - State Archives Collection.

[71] Wiblin. 56.

[72] *Bathurst Free Press and Mining Journal*. 1853. 'Family Notices', 22 January 1853. National Library of Australia. 3. http://nla.gov.au/nla.news-article62047118.

[73] Backler, Joseph. n.d. *[Bathurst], c.1847-57 / Painted by Joseph Backler? (Digitised by Mitchell Library, State Library of New South Wales)*. State Library of New South Wales. Accessed 6 April 2022. https://collection.sl.nsw.gov.au/record/nmQdbvRn/2BNaKJlA8VdbB.

Caroline saw the infant township form when the government lifted the ban on settlers living west of the river. People who had been granted land were now able to occupy their grants and the town swelled in response. Settlers like William Lane packed up their families and started building their permanent homes.[74] Caroline, however, didn't stay long and was re-assigned to a ticket of leave holder named James Dauber.

[74] William Lane built Orton Park see NSW Land Registry Services. 2023. 'County: Bathurst, Parish: Bathurst, Sheet 1, Edition 6'. Historical Lands Records Viewer. 2023. https://hlrv.nswlrs.com.au/.

CHAPTER 3
JAMES DAUBER

Twelve years prior to Caroline being assigned to James Dauber or Dawber as he was sometimes referred to, he had found himself in a Lancashire court, accused of breaking into a Liverpool linen draper's house and stealing linen, lace, and cotton goods.[75] Found guilty and sentenced to death he was fortunate, to have his sentence commuted to transportation for life.

He was sent to the *York* prison hulk where he waited for a ship to take him to the colonies. That ship was the *Hindostan (I)* and he was put on board at 8.30pm on the 13th of July 1821 with one hundred and fifty one other convicts. The efficient loading operation was overseen by the twenty-eight military guards from the 30th, 48th and 69th regiments who had boarded the ship earlier in the day. There were also five women and six children on board.

At 8am on the 29th of July they finally set sail from Spithead.

The ship's doctor recorded onboard events that he deemed noteworthy. One event was recorded for James on the 9th of August when he was "released from irons…for good conduct."[76] Overall it was an unremarkable journey taking just over four months.

Like the women of the *Fanny,* the convicts were mustered on the deck of the ship on arrival in Sydney Harbour. In this case each man was issued a complete outfit, including a Kersey Jacket, Kersey Waistcoat, Raven-duck trousers, three shirts, two pairs of stockings, a pair of shoes, a woollen cap, and a neck handkerchief.[77]

The prisoners walked under armed guard to the convict barracks to await distribution to either private settlers or to work on government projects. On the 15th of February 1822 James was assigned to Patt Moore and was working at Petersham, but after ten days he was transferred to Joseph Furness at the Georges River.[78] James worked for Joseph for over a year before being returned to the Barracks on the 19th of July 1823.[79]

---

[75] *Westmorland Gazette*. 1821. 'Lancaster Assizes', 7 April 1821. British Newspaper Archive. 3. https://www.britishnewspaperarchive.co.uk/viewer/bl/0000399/18210407/009/0003.

[76] Evans, William. 1821. 'Royal Navy Medical Journals, 1817-1856. H. Hindostan. 25 Jun 1821-29 Nov 1821. Image 8'. Ancestry. Accessed 12 April 2022. https://www.ancestry.com.au.

[77] 'New South Wales, Australia, Colonial Secretary's Papers, 1788-1856. Special Bundles, 1794-1825. Image 6198.' 1821. Ancestry. Accessed 12 April 2022. https://www.ancestry.com.au.

[78] 'New South Wales, Australia, Colonial Secretary's Papers, 1788-1856. Special Bundles, 1794-1825. Image 2943.' 1822. Ancestry. Accessed 12 April 2022. https://www.ancestry.com.au.

[79] 'New South Wales, Australia, Colonial Secretary's Papers, 1788-1856, Special Bundles, 1794-1825. Image 2946'. 1823. Accessed 23 July 2023. https://www.ancestry.com.au.

Figure 11: Male convict clothing[80]

Figure 12: Convict Barracks Sydney 1820[81]

[80] Part of image from: Charmichael, John. 1829. *Item 05: Sydney from Woolloomooloo Hill.* Mitchell Library, State Library of New South Wales. Accessed 10 May 2024. https://collection.sl.nsw.gov.au/record/1l4lyNV1/bJAAg6J2pE2Ol.

[81] *Collection of Views Predominantly of Sydney, Liverpool, and the Sunda Straits, and Portraits, ca 1807, 1829-1847, 1887.(5) Convict Barrack Sydney N.S. Wales*. 1820. State Library of New South Wales. Accessed 12 April 2022. https://collection.sl.nsw.gov.au/record/16AJqGqn/4NOW6xjk4kMO0.

James was then transferred to the nascent convict settlement in Wellington Valley on the traditional lands of the Wiradyuri people. It was located at the colony's remote 'limits of location,' situated about one-hundred-and-sixty kilometres northwest of Bathurst. The settlement was under the charge of Lieutenant Percy Simpson, who not only had to manage the convicts but also the day-to-day operations which included the agricultural endeavours to produce food.

James joined the ranks of eighty men engaged in a variety of essential tasks:

> *ploughing and sowing, thrashing and grinding wheat, baking bricks, burning lime, repairing carts, yolks and farm implements or felling trees to be hauled to the settlement for posts, rails and panels.*[82]

In such a remote location, the convicts:

> *could exercise considerable power in their relationship with their masters...they were idle and insubordinate, feigned illness, pilfered food, smuggled and distilled liquor. They sabotaged the construction of buildings and the ploughing of fields. They burnt wheat stacks, drove away livestock, waylaid the supply carts and destroyed accounts.*[83]

Despite the volatile situation there were over three hundred acres of land under cultivation and forty public buildings constructed in less than three years. The government stock station that supplied meat to the convicts was established about sixteen kilometres away and was manned by more trusted convicts. Consisting of an overseer, three stockmen and a clerk.[84]

Figure 13: The Stockman[85]

---

[82] Roberts, David Andrew. 2000. '"A Sort of Inland Norfolk Island"? Isolation, Coercion and Resistance on the Wellington Valley Convict Station, 1823-26'. *Journal of Australian Colonial History* 2 (1): 50–73. 58. 'A sort of inland Norfolk Island'?: Isolation, coercion and resistance on the Wellington Valley Convict Station, 1823-26 | Journal of Australian Colonial History (slv.vic.gov.au)

[83] Ibid. 59.

[84] Maxwell, John. 1982. Letters of John Maxwell, Superintendent of Government Stock, 1823-31. Wangaratta, Victoria: Shoestring Press. 50

[85] Gill, Samuel Thomas. n.d. *Samuel Thomas Gill Original Sketches, 1844-1866. 38. [The Stockman]*. Mitchell Library, State Library of New South Wales. Accessed 12 April 2022. https://collection.sl.nsw.gov.au/digital/eDwQ0yj7oK4b.

Within eight months of arriving James had earnt enough trust with Simpson that he was sent to Bathurst to pick up a load of cattle. Simpson wrote to the Commandant at Bathurst, Major Morrisett:

> *As this Settlement will soon be in want of meat rations I send a very well and valued man named Dauber...to get what quantity of cattle for rations you may be pleased to order here. Lent as there are no horses belonging to this Settlement it will be necessary; they should be sent as heretofore by mounted stockmen from Bathurst to accompany Dauber.*[86]

With the commandant's letter tucked in his pocket he set off on his long walk on the 27th of March 1824. It was a time when most Europeans felt unsafe traveling the roads alone. The Wiradyuri people had been carrying out Giban (payback)[87] against the stockmen between Molong and Vittoria, since October the previous year. The retaliation was in response to an armed pursuit by the stockmen the previous year. The stockmen had been instructed by William Lawson to pursue the Wiradyuri. for killing the cattle. He armed them and sent them off. No report of their actions was made but the Wiradyuri response was to return and kill two of the stockmen.[88] Traditional justice.

Just five days before James departed the stockmen at Swallow Creek had been stripped and tied up in their hut. One had managed to get to the nearby overseer and military detachment calling for help. When they arrived, the conflict escalated and two Wiradyuri were killed and three were arrested.[89]

James arrived safely at Bathurst probably because he wasn't a stockman and had not committed any offence that warranted Giban. It is also possible that he may have had a Wiradyuri guide for the trip as they were known to accompany white travellers and the Wiradyuri people around Wellington Valley were noted as being "on terms of perfect amity" with the Settlement.[90]

When he started the return trip on the 20th of April there was a lull in the hostilities, which was fortunate considering he was accompanied by stockmen.[91] They arrived without incident.

---

[86] 'New South Wales, Australia, Colonial Secretary's Papers. Main Series of Letters Received, 1788-1826. Simpson to Morisett. Image 25233-25234'. 1824. Ancestry. Accessed 13 April 2022. https://www.ancestry.com.au.

[87] 'Gudyarra (War/Battle with Spears)'. 2024. Dhuluny. Accessed 3 July 2024. https://www.dhuluny.com.au/gudyarra-war-battle-with-spears.

[88] 'New South Wales, Australia, Colonial Secretary's Papers. Main Series of Letters Received, 1788-1826. Maxwell to Goulburn. Image 24935'. 1823. Ancestry. Accessed 13 April 2022. https://www.ancestry.com.au..

[89] 'New South Wales, Australia, Colonial Secretary's Papers. Main Series of Letters Received, 1788-1826. Depositions of John Softly and John Epstien. Image 25217'. 1824. Ancestry. Accessed 13 April 2022. https://www.ancestry.com.au.

[90] *Sydney Gazette and New South Wales Advertiser.* 14 Oct 1824. 'SUPREME COURT, SATURDAY, OCT. 10.' Accessed 3 July 2024. 2. http://nla.gov.au/nla.news-article2183288.

[91] 'New South Wales, Australia, Colonial Secretary's Papers. Main Series of Letters Received, 1788-1826. Morrisett to Goulburn. Image 25230'. 1824. Ancestry. Accessed 13 April 2022. https://www.ancestry.com.au.

Figure 14: Wellington Valley, New South Wales, looking east from Government House 1826[92]

On the 14th of August Governor Brisbane declared martial law against all Aboriginal people west of Mount York. It stated:

> *Bloodshed may be stopped by the Use of Arms against the Natives beyond the ordinary Rule of Law in Time of Peace; and, for this End, Resort to summary Justice has become necessary.[93]*

The proclamation effectively gave the white population the approval to shoot any Wiradyuri they came across. It opened the door to massacres.

The frontier war between the Wiradyuri and the colonisers around Bathurst did not appear to break out at Wellington Valley. Although cattle continued disappearing this was the result of convict actions. It may be that the subversive actions of the convicts at Wellington Valley were seen by the Wiradyuri as an assistance to their cause to get rid of the colonisers. They may even have been the beneficiaries after the cattle were lost, gaining an abundant meat source.

Six months after his return from Bathurst James was feeling confident enough with his knowledge of the area that he chose to abscond.[94] He remained at large for over four months before returning to Wellington Valley.[95] Absconding was the:

> *principal and preferred means of convict resistance. [It]was, a powerful tool of subversion in a situation where an absence could seriously disable a fledgling settlement. Not surprisingly it was one of the most severely punished offences at Wellington.[96]*

---

[92]Earle, Augustus. 1826. *Wellington Valley, New South Wales, Looking East from Government House [Picture]*. Watercolour. National Library of Australia. Accessed 16 April 2022. https://nla.gov.au/nla.obj-134496732.

[93] *Sydney Gazette and New South Wales Advertiser*. 19 Aug 1824. 'NEW SOUTH WALES.' Accessed 4 July 2024.1. http://nla.gov.au/nla.news-article2183147.

[94]*Sydney Gazette and New South Wales Advertiser*. 1824. 'Extracts from the Latest London Journals.', 14 October 1824. National Library of Australia. 4. http://nla.gov.au/nla.news-article2183282.

[95]*Sydney Gazette and New South Wales Advertiser*. 1825. 'PRINCIPAL SUPERINTENDRNT'S OFFICE. SYDNEY, JANUARY 25, 1825.', 27 January 1825. National Library of Australia. 1. http://nla.gov.au/nla.news-article2183659.

[96] Roberts, David Andrew. 2000. '"A Sort of Inland Norfolk Island"?: Isolation, Coercion and Resistance on the Wellington Valley Convict Station, 1823-26'. *Journal of Australian Colonial History* 2 (1): 50–73. https://doi.org/10.3316/ielapa.200011056.

As a runaway convict ranging in the bush, he was also officially a bushranger. Bushrangers were typically unarmed; however, it wasn't long before they started employing arms in robberies.[97]James along with many convicts at the settlement chose to run away at various times. They were not afraid of the Wiradyuri when they went bush which again points to a tolerance. Any trust he had earned with Simpson should have evaporated after he absconded, however later in the year he was sent to Sydney for provisions.[98]

In 1826, John Maxwell made the move from Bathurst to Wellington to take charge of the Government stock station. Concurrently, due to its "inaccessible and economically unviable"[99]nature, the activities of the convict settlement underwent a temporary reduction before being revived as a facility for housing educated convicts considered unfit for manual labour and deemed troublesome.

James retained his role as a carter, and by 1828, his accumulated local expertise led to his selection as a servant to accompany Captain Charles Sturt on his first journey of discovery into the uncharted interior regions of the colony.

---

[97]Cumpston, J.H.L. 1951. *Charles Sturt - His Life and Journeys of Exploration*. Project Gutenberg. https://gutenberg.net.au/ebooks07/0700391h.html#ch3.

[98] 'New South Wales, Census and Population Books, Wellington Valley Population Book. Image 8.' 1825. Ancestry. Accessed 13 April 2022. https://www.ancestry.com.au.

[99] Roberts, David Andrew. 2006. '"The Valley of Swells" "Special" or "Educated" Convicts on the Wellington Valley Settlement, 1827–1830'. *History Australia* 3 (1): 11.10. https://doi.org/10.2104/ha060011.

CHAPTER 4
JOURNEY OF DISCOVERY

There was a mystery that needed solving and Captain Charles Sturt decided he was the man for the job. Was there an inland sea that all the interior rivers flowed into? Explorer, John Oxley had followed the flooded Macquarie River back in 1817, only to be stopped by impassable marshes and reeds. He had formulated the hypothesis of an inland sea.

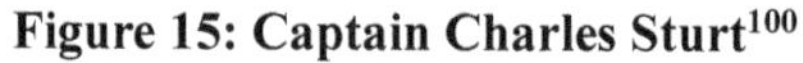

Figure 15: Captain Charles Sturt[100]

Thirty-three-year-old Sturt, a career military officer, approached Governor Darling with a proposal to pursue the Macquarie and Castlereagh Rivers to ascertain their true conclusions. Given the fact that the land had been in drought since 1826 it was thought he had a good chance of getting through the marshes.

Figure 16: Hamilton Hume in later life[101]

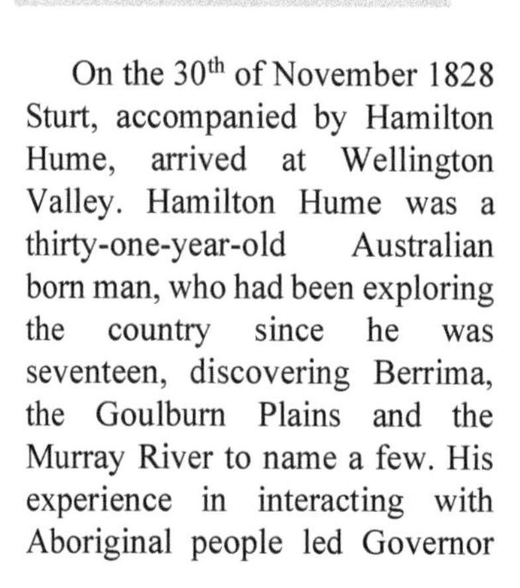

On the 30th of November 1828 Sturt, accompanied by Hamilton Hume, arrived at Wellington Valley. Hamilton Hume was a thirty-one-year-old Australian born man, who had been exploring the country since he was seventeen, discovering Berrima, the Goulburn Plains and the Murray River to name a few. His experience in interacting with Aboriginal people led Governor

[100] *Captain Charles Sturt [Picture]*. 1895. National Library of Australia. Accessed 16 April 2022. https://nla.gov.au/nla.obj-136105796.

[101] A'Beckett, Edward. 1881. *Hamilton Hume F.R.G.S, Explorer*. State Library of Victoria. Accessed 16 April 2022. http://handle.slv.vic.gov.au/10381/303380.

Darling to include him in the expedition.

Upon their arrival at Wellington Valley, the final preparations were made. Provisions for six months were sent by the deputy Commissary General, along with "arms and ammunition, with rockets for signals, and an ample supply of simple medicines."[102]

Table 1: Exploration Supplies List

Equipment	Tools	Gear for repairs	Gear for the men	Gear for food	Travel & Navigation
2 Tents	2 Felling-axes	2 lb. Pack thread	10 Knives	2 Frying pans	1 Boat compass
9 Harness casks	4 Tomahawks	24 Needles	10 Forks	2 Tinder boxes	1 Telescope
23 Canvas bags	2 Hammers	1/4 lb. Bristles	10 Spoons	2 Tea kettles (tin)	1 Spare glass for telescope
4 Tin cases	1 Handsaw	7 lbs. Leather	10 Tin pots	1 Flour sieve	1 Tin case (for charts)
16 Padlocks	3 Billhooks	1/2 lb. Thread	4 Razors	4 Iron pots, (camp kettles)	1 Hack saddle
7 Tarpaulins	3 Awls	24 Sets horseshoes	4 Brushes	100 Fishhooks (large)	1 Bridle
10 Haversacks	3 Broad hoes	2000 Horse nails	4 Combs	12 Fishing lines	14 Pack saddles
113 Fathoms one-inch rope	1 Hammer Blacksmith's	Pitch and oil	10 Tin dishes	3 Water breakers	14 Pairs hobbles
113 Fathoms 1 1/2-inch rope	1 Paring knife	Hemp or twine	8 Jackets		1 Pair of steelyards
1 Boat with sail and oars	2 Chipping knife		8 Duck frocks		2 Bullock collars
1 Boat carriage	2 Rasps		8 Shirts		2 Bullock backbands & pipes
1 Canvass boat cover	1 Pair pincers		16 Trousers		2 Leading cruppers
	1 Cutter		24 Pair shoes		
	1 Pair scissors		16 Blankets		
			16 Pair stockings		

Conversions:
1 Fathom = 1.8288 metres
1 inch = 2.54cm
1lb (pound) = 0.453592 kg

---

[102] Sturt, Charles. 2004. *Two Expeditions into the Interior of Southern Australia*. Project Gutenberg. Appendix 1.https://www.gutenberg.org/files/4330/4330-h/4330-h.htm#ap1.1.

Sturt wrote:

> *on the 5th, our preparations being wholly completed, and the loads arranged, the party was mustered, and was found to consist of myself and Mr. Hume, two soldiers and eight prisoners of the crown, two of whom were to return with dispatches. Our animals numbered two riding, and seven pack, horses, two draft, and eight pack, bullocks, exclusive of two horses of my own, and two for the men to be sent back.*[103]

The convicts chosen alongside James were Samuel Henwood[104], James Norman[105], Peter Snow[106], William Bryant[107], Stephen Peck[108], Owen Reilly[109], James Smith[110] and John Williams.[111] Picked for their skills as a carpenter, a harness maker, a horse shoer, and stockmen. James Dauber served as the overseer of stock. It seems plausible from the equipment list that the men's sizes may have been a factor in their selection also. The list simply states 8 shirts, 8 duck frocks, 16 pairs of trousers and so forth without any distinction of sizes. A sure indication that it was one size fits all, even down to their 24 pairs of shoes. They were going to do a lot of walking.

Looking at the ticket of leave records, James Dauber was the tallest at 5-foot 11½ inches and Stephen Peck was the shortest at 5 foot 6 inches. Most of the men were close to 5 foot 8 inches. So, either James found everything was a bit tight or everyone else found the clothes and shoes a bit big. They did have needles, thread and leather so could have made alterations as needed.

Also on the expedition were three soldiers named Spencer, Fraser and Hopkinson along with Sturt's man servant Harris.

On the 7th of December the expedition commenced its journey. Setting off in the afternoon to avoid the worst of the summer heat, the pack animals were laden with supplies, including a boat.

Their initial objective was to reach Mount Harris and it took them almost two weeks to get there. They covered two hundred kilometres in the scorching heat. Temperatures were recorded up to 129°F (53°C) in the shade and 149°F (65°C) in the sun. The stress of the heat combined with their wandering livestock posed significant challenges along the way and resulted in both Henwood and Williams

---

103 Sturt, Charles. 2004, Ch1.

104 'New South Wales, Australia, Tickets of Leave, 1810-1869, for Samuel Henwood. (NRS 12202), May1829-Dec 1829. Image 223'. n.d. Ancestry. Accessed 16 April 2022. https://www.ancestry.com.au.

105 'New South Wales, Australia, Tickets of Leave, 1810-1869 for James Norman. (NRS 12202), May1829-Dec 1829. Image 224'. n.d. Ancestry. Accessed 16 April 2022. https://www.ancestry.com.au.

106 'New South Wales, Australia, Tickets of Leave, 1810-1869 for Peter Snow. (NRS 12202), May1829-Dec 1829. Image 225'. n.d. Ancestry. Accessed 16 April 2022. https://www.ancestry.com.au.

107 'New South Wales, Australia, Tickets of Leave, 1810-1869 for William Bryant. (NRS 12202), May1829-Dec 1829. Image 226'. n.d. Ancestry. Accessed 16 April 2022. https://www.ancestry.com.au.

108 'New South Wales, Australia, Tickets of Leave, 1810-1869 for Stephen Peck. (NRS 12202), May1829-Dec 1829. Image 228'. n.d. Ancestry. Accessed 16 April 2022. https://www.ancestry.com.au.

109 'New South Wales, Australia, Tickets of Leave, 1810-1869 for Owen Reilly. (NRS 12202), May1829-Dec 1829. Image 229'. n.d. Ancestry. Accessed 16 April 2022. https://www.ancestry.com.au.

110 'New South Wales, Australia, Tickets of Leave, 1810-1869 for James Smith. (NRS 12202), May1829-Dec 1829. Image 230'. n.d. Ancestry. Accessed 16 April 2022. https://www.ancestry.com.au.

111 'New South Wales, Australia, Tickets of Leave, 1810-1869 for John Williams. (NRS 12202), May1829-Dec 1829. Image 231'. n.d. Ancestry. Accessed 16 April 2022. https://www.ancestry.com.au.

suffering "a painful irritation of the eyes, which were dreadfully blood-shot and weak."[112] John Williams' chestnut eyes were so inflamed that Sturt thought he needed to bleed him. They rested for a day. Then after travelling the next day in the sun, "not only had they a return of inflammation, but several other of the men"[113] were also afflicted.

Christmas day found them camped along the Macquarie River, seven hours west of Mount Harris. The following morning, Spencer and Reilly were dispatched back to Wellington Valley with letters updating the Governor on their progress. They were instructed to return to Mount Harris with necessary supplies and further instructions.

Pressing on, the expedition headed in a north by northwest direction, crossing a plain until reaching the Macquarie Marshes. Blocked and unable to proceed, they backtracked to the river where Sturt decided to divide the group. He, planned to take two men and follow the river in the boat, while Hume and another pair were to venture north and explore the extent of the marshes. Each group carried provisions for a week.

Figure 17: Macquarie Marshes 10 November 1947[114]

[112] Sturt, Charles, 2004. Ch.1.

[113] Sturt, Charles, 2004. Ch1.

[114] *Birds at Macquarie Marshes (Warren) Western N.S.W. Image 27.* 1947. Photograph. Mitchell Library, State Library of New South Wales and Courtesy ACP Magazines Ltd. Accessed 17 April 2022. https://collection.sl.nsw.gov.au/record/Yj7oAdD9.

The remaining men stayed at the camp, with James overseeing the stock. It was:

hot and suffocating [and they] were tormented by myriads of mosquitoes, but the waters were perfectly sweet to the taste...the birds, ...together with the frogs, made incessant noises around [them].[115]

Hume and Sturt reconvened at the camp within two days, sharing their findings. Hume believed he had found the exit of the Macquarie River from the marshes, so the party packed up camp, but on reaching the supposed exit they found their path blocked again by the reeds.

Sturt again split the party into two to look for the Macquarie's true path. Leaving on the last day of the year in the extreme heat, Hume went scouting to the northeast, with James and one of the other men, while Sturt took two men with him on a northwest path.

Sturt travelled 200km through dry and hot conditions, until the sun exposure became too much. He and the men were severely sunburned, with blisters on their faces and severely cracked lips. The pain in their eyes was so severe that even looking towards the setting sun was impossible. Sturt had not found the Macquarie River again, and from the vantage of the outcrop where he stood, he "could not trace either the windings of a stream, or the course of a mountain torrent."[116]

Backtracking from the outcrop which he named Oxley's Tableland, the group passed back over the two creeks they had found, making use of the water.[117]

On meeting Hume's group back at camp Sturt wrote that:

soon after his [Hume's] arrival, Dawber, my overseer of animals... was taken suddenly ill. During the night he became much worse, with shivering and spasms, and on the following morning he was extremely weak and feverish. To add to my anxiety, Mr. Hume also complained of indisposition... I ordered the tents to be struck, and placing Dawber on my horse, we all moved.[118]

The two explorers compared notes. Hume reported he had crossed a range on New Year's Day, calling it New Year's Range but conceded he had not found the Macquarie's path. They decided there was a remote possibility that it lay between their two routes and wanting a definitive answer they decided to go on.

Before starting Sturt wanted to find out if Spencer and Reilly had returned to Mount Harris with their provisions and further instructions, so he returned to Mount Harris. He wrote that:

Mr. Hume was too unwell for me to think of imposing additional fatigue upon him; I left him, therefore, to conduct the party, by easy stages, to the northward, until such time as I should overtake them. Even in one day there was a visible improvement in the men, and Dawber's attack seemed to be rather the effects of cold than of anything else. A death, however, under our circumstances, would have been so truly deplorable an event, that the least illness was sufficient to create alarm.[119]

---

[115] Sturt, Charles, 2004, Ch.1.

[116] Ibid.

[117] He crossed the creek now known as the Bogan River near present day Gongolgon and Marra Creek.

[118] Sturt, Charles, 2004, Ch.1.

[119] Ibid

Sturt re-joined the party having found no one at Mount Harris and the group continued their northward path. They couldn't find the exit of the Macquarie and concluded it just loses its flow in the marshes.

From here they again crossed to New Year's Range and setup camp on the nearby creek they named New Year's Creek.[120] Sturt and Hume went off exploring whilst James stayed at camp to mind the stock.

The men took it in turns watching over the stock and on the first evening it was Norman's turn. He was sitting astride one of the horses when he spotted a kangaroo. Emboldened by being on the horse he thought he would have a go at catching it. He crossed the creek but soon found night had set in and he was lost.

James realised he was missing and set out searching. He took the last riding horse and set off following the tracks left by Norman's horse. He searched all day before thirst drove him back to camp. Sturt and Hume had returned as had Norman's horse, but there was no sign of the man himself.

A plan was hatched to set the bush alight that night in the hopes Norman would see it and return. It worked. He made his way into camp tired, hungry and most of all thirsty, after three nights and two days, without water or food.

After a couple of days' rest a new plan was formulated. They were going to follow New Year's Creek. Travelling north the creek's flow gradually lessened. Day after day it disappeared.

> *We passed hollow after hollow that had successively dried up, although originally of considerable depth; and, when we at length found water, it was doubtful how far we could make use of it. Sometimes in boiling it left a sediment nearly equal to half its body; at other times it was so bitter as to be quite unpalatable. That on which we subsisted was scraped up from small puddles, heated by the sun's rays; and so uncertain were we of finding water at the end of the day's journey, that we were obliged to carry a supply on one of the bullocks. There was scarcely a living creature, even of the feathered race, to be seen to break the stillness of the forest. The native dogs alone wandered about, though they had scarcely strength to avoid us; and their melancholy howl, breaking in upon the ear at the dead of the night, only served to impress more fully on the mind the absolute loneliness of the desert.*[121]

---

[120] The Bogan River.

[121] Sturt, Charles, 2004. Ch1.

Figure 18: The Bogan River (New Year's Creek).[122]

The creek bed continued meandering towards Oxley's Tableland until it took a sudden bend east. Sturt wanted to keep going west and ordered the group to the waterhole he knew was at the base of Oxley's Tableland. They travelled over baking open country, finally reaching the waterhole where the suffering stock and horses "rushed into it."[123];

Camp was set up and the men and animals left to rest for three days while Sturt, Hume, Hopkinson and the tinker went on another side trip to the southwest. They returned secure in the knowledge that the only courses of action now were to either follow New Year's Creek, or to retreat; Sturt was not willing to give up at this point so they set of across country, intending to meet up with the creek to their north. When they reached the river, they almost didn't recognise it. The channel was much larger with higher banks but, to their dismay it was completely dry. They set up camp and desperate for water Sturt kept looking:

to my joy, I found a pond of water within a hundred yards of the tents. It is impossible for me to describe the relief I felt at this success, or the gladness it spread among the men.[124]

[122] *Sketch on the Bogan River*. 1870. State Library of Victoria. Accessed 3 May 2024. http://handle.slv.vic.gov.au/10381/252354.

[123] Ibid.

[124] Sturt, Charles. 2004. Ch.2.

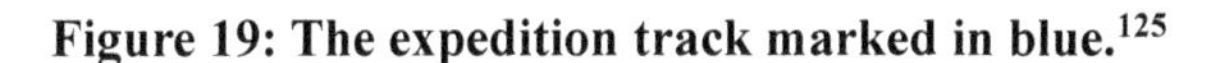

Figure 19: The expedition track marked in blue.[125]

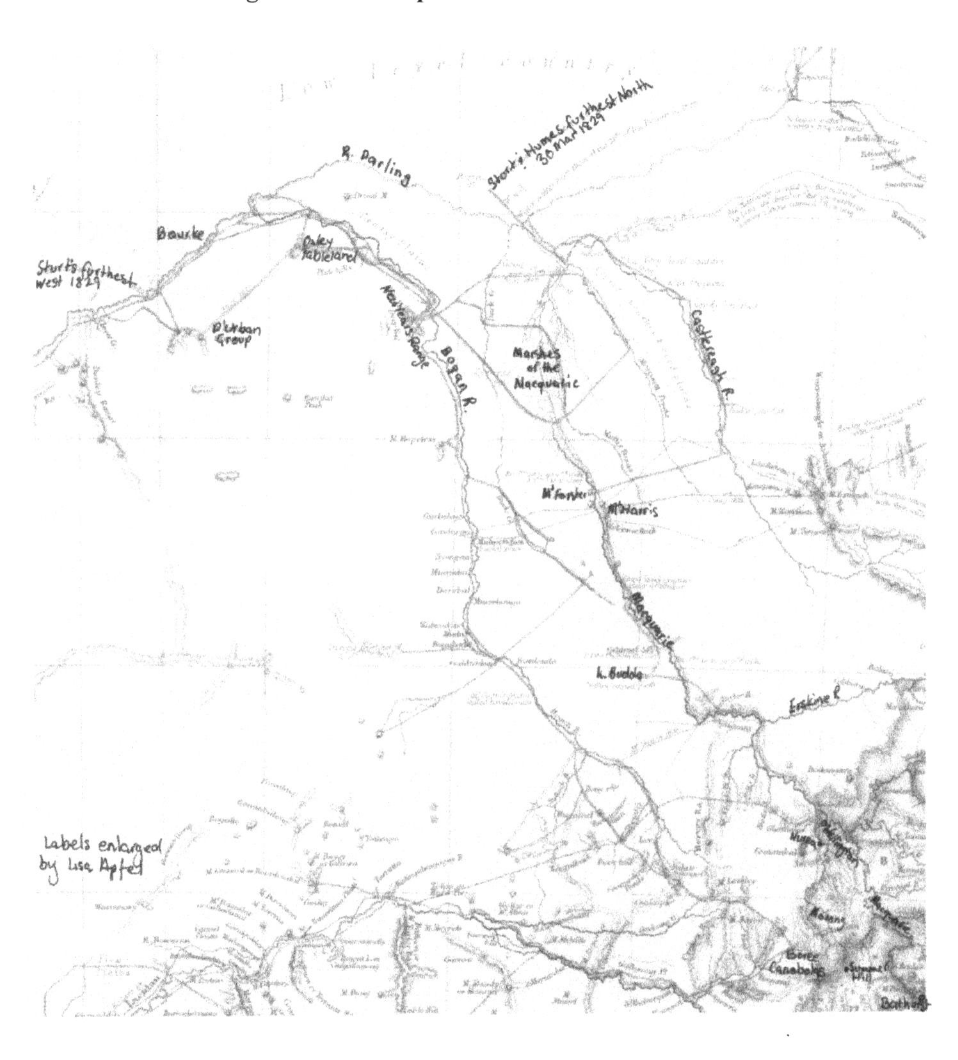

Desperate days were spent looking for more water, but when none was found, they decided to follow some tracks left by the local Barkindji people. Within a mile they suddenly come across the "banks of a noble river."[126] Known as the Baarka by the Barkindji, Sturt named it the Darling River.

Its banks were about twelve to thirteen metres high and its channel between sixty and seventy-five metres wide. The water level was low, but it was a magnet to pelicans and other birds. Sturt wrote:

---

[125] Part of the map: Arrowsmith, John. 1838. 'The South Eastern Portion of Australia Compiled from the Colonial Surveys, and from Details Furnished by Exploration Expeditions John Arrowsmith'. London. National Library of Australia. Accessed 11 April 2022. https://nla.gov.au/nla.obj-230630599.

[126] Ibid.

our surprise and delight may better be imagined than described. Our difficulties seemed to be at an end, for here was a river that promised to reward all our exertions...Its banks were too precipitous to allow of our watering the cattle, but the men eagerly descended to quench their thirst, which a powerful sun had contributed to increase; nor shall I ever forget the cry of amazement that followed their doing so, or the looks of terror and disappointment with which they called out to inform me that the water was so salt as to be unfit to drink! ... the discovery was certainly a blow for which I was not prepared. Our hopes were annihilated at the moment of their apparent realization.[127]

They followed the river and concluded that the salt was coming from brine springs in the riverbed. With no prospect of fresh water, it was a matter of survival that they return to Mount Harris.

Reaching Mount Harris they could see a newly built hut. Three men came out and including Reilly. Relief swept through the expedition, knowing they would have bought supplies. The other two men were a soldier and a draymen. They had been there for four weeks and in addition to the supplies they had more cattle and news.

Sturt set about planning to track the Castlereagh River. They departed on the 7th of March, with Boyle replacing Norman. They took three days to travel almost a hundred kilometres[128] and found this river was empty, like all the others. Sturt wrote it "damped the spirits and ardour of the men."[129] They followed the course of the river and after almost two weeks they "all had a depression of spirits."[130] It took six more days to meet up with the Darling River. There was no mistaking it. It was as large and salty as before. Sturt finally decided to return to Wellington Valley. They arrived on the 21st of April, four and a half months after leaving.

Sturt regarded the expedition as a success and attributed it to the conduct of the men. He noted that they were intelligent, persevering and had even tempers.

They had discovered the Bogan and Darling Rivers and proven that there was no inland sea. The convicts:

behaved, on all occasions, as steadily as it was possible for men to do...The success of an expedition depends so much on the conduct of the persons of whom it is composed, that too much attention cannot be given to the selection even of the most subordinate.[131]

After the expedition was completed James and all the other convicts went back to their designated convict duties. For James that meant resuming his work at Wellington Valley.

On the cusp of turning thirty he had been serving his sentence for eight years. His twenties had been forfeited and he was still single with no family. Then two months after his return from the expedition he was granted his ticket of leave on the 30th of June 1829. It was granted "in consideration of his good conduct while

---

[127] Sturt, Charles, 2004, Ch.2.

[128] Near present day Coonamble

[129] Sturt, Charles, 2004. Ch3.

[130] Ibid.

[131] Sturt, Charles. 2004. Ch.6.

employed in a tour of discovery under Captain Sturt."[132] A condition of the ticket of leave was that he had to remain in the Bathurst district, which in 1829 included Wellington Valley. It also required that he report regularly to local authorities and attend divine worship every Sunday. The last requirement was an impossibility with no minister in the area.

Like James, the other convicts of the expedition were granted their tickets of leave on the same day. Samuel Henwood a blacksmith and sailor by trade was required to remain in the Liverpool district,[133] as were James Norman, a brickmaker,[134] and Peter Snow, a farmer.[135]William Bryant,[136] Owen Reilly[137]and James Smith,[138] labourers, Stephen Peck, a groom and pedlar,[139]and John Williams, a sailor,[140] were to remain in the Bathurst district just like James.

The Wellington Valley convict settlement was disbanded in March 1830 and the stock station was also wound down, with stock being sold to surrounding squatters or sent back over the mountains to Emu Plains and Mulgoa. By the middle of 1831, the last remnants of the Wellington Valley stores were left under the watch of Assistant Superintendent Bennet.[141]

James who was working for himself soon heard the news that the stores were being closed because the missionaries were arriving. Reverends Handt and Watson after reaching Bathurst had continued on to Wellington Valley, where they set about their work, setting-up the new Aboriginal Mission. They hoped to convert all Aboriginal people to Christianity. They also intended to minister to Europeans they met on their travels.

With his ticket of leave secured, James would have had no trouble finding work. His skills as an overseer and farmer[142] and his local knowledge were invaluable to the new settlers. He was soon located between Neurea and Mumbil about one hundred and thirty kilometres north-west of Bathurst. He built a hut and decided that he wanted a wife and family.

For a man in his situation the opportunities to find a wife were rare. Men dominated the population, and the local Wiradyuri women were often the victims of this imbalance. James however decided to approach getting a wife a bit differently and applied to the Female Factory for a domestic servant.

---

[132] 'New South Wales, Australia, Tickets of Leave, 1810-1869 for James Dauber. (NRS12202), May1829-Dec 1829. Image 227'. n.d. Ancestry. Accessed 7 April 2022. https://www.ancestry.com.au.

[133] 'New South Wales, Australia, Tickets of Leave, 1810-1869 for Samuel Henwood.

[134] 'New South Wales, Australia, Tickets of Leave, 1810-1869 for James Norman.

[135]'New South Wales, Australia, Tickets of Leave, 1810-1869 for Peter Snow.

[136] 'New South Wales, Australia, Tickets of Leave, 1810-1869 for William Bryant.

[137] 'New South Wales, Australia, Tickets of Leave, 1810-1869 for Owen Reilly. ((NRS 12202), May 1829-Dec 1829, Image 416'. n.d. Ancestry. Accessed 15 August 2023. https://www.ancestry.com.au.

[138] 'New South Wales, Australia, Tickets of Leave, 1810-1869 for James Smith.

[139] 'New South Wales, Australia, Tickets of Leave, 1810-1869 for Stephen Peck.

[140] 'New South Wales, Australia, Tickets of Leave, 1810-1869 for John Williams.

[141] 'The Wellington Valley Project,' Wellpro Directory. Bennett, Henry A.B.

[142] 'New South Wales, Australia, Tickets of Leave, 1810-1869 for James Dauber.

Journeying to Bathurst he approached Matron Black and applied for a female servant. He was assigned Caroline. He must have been ecstatic, and she must have been terrified.

CHAPTER 5
CAROLINE AND JAMES

Caroline found herself thrust into the unknown, compelled to journey alongside a stranger. A rare feat for a white woman, she embarked on a trip that only a handful of white people had undertaken, traversing the expansive lands of the Wiradyuri nation. Her isolation would have been profound, vulnerability palpable, and solitude all-encompassing, with only this man by her side.

Departing Bathurst Caroline and James travelled the "very rugged road."[143] They ascended the summit of the range of hills to the west of the Macquarie where they could look back over the Bathurst Plains and see the "vast garden of agriculture, and...the rapid progress of the march of civilization."[144] They travelled west towards Kings Plains (near present day Blayney) where Caroline may have felt like LI who wrote that,

> *we felt that we were leaving the abodes of industry and civilization, to penetrate the interminable wilds of the interior, the dominion of the sable sons of nature; but these gloomy reflections were soon dissipated as we came to Evans' Plains... A finer tract of land cannot possibly be conceived, thinly wooded, watered by numberless creeks, and affording rich pasture for the most extensive herds. King's Plains are swampy, and have been generally, and are now chiefly located for the depasturing of cattle. During the period of hostilities with the natives in 1824, this vicinity was the scene of much bloodshed. The atrocities of these misguided people on that occasion, called forth the most active measures of the local authorities, in which nearly all the respectable settlers of the district joined, under the direction of the then Commandant, Colonel Morisset. Before the termination of hostilities, martial law being in full operation, the slaughter was dreadful, but the result decidedly proved the good policy of the course adopted, for since that time the most amicable feeling has subsisted between the Aboriginal and Anglo-Australians. At the distance of thirty-two miles from Bathurst, is a Government stock station, also a military post known by the names of Summer Hill and Frederick's Valley [Lucknow]. We found nothing worthy of remark at this place, which formed our first stage, and early the next morning journied (sic) forward for some miles, through a level country, which appears subject to floods, and of a rank soil: droves of kangaroos were nipping the dew-bespeckled grass; their number about one particular spot, twelve miles from Summer Hill, has given it the name of Kangaroo Bay*

[143] 'The Wellington Valley Project,' Watson's Journal.

[144] *Sydney Gazette and New South Wales Advertiser*. 19 Jan 1832. 'AN EXCURSION FROM BATHURST TO WELLINGTON VALLEY.' Accessed 5 July 2024. 3. http://nla.gov.au/nla.news-article2204528.

[Kangaroobie], and, in like manner, Emu Swamp [Orange]. Crossing several deep creeks, which in wet weather are for days together impassable, Molong Plains appeared before us, also a cattle station, protected by a military picquet. At the distance of a mile from Molong is Copper Hill, where some fine specimens of that mineral have been found. The road to Boorai [Boree] branches off at this place, and Mount Lachlan ; or, as the three lofty peaks are more familiarly called, the Canobolas, elevate their summits almost to the clouds. Our course now lay through a fine champaign country, agreeably diversified with gentle undulations of hill and dale. A pretty sheet of water, called Larry's Lake [Larras Lee], intersects the road, crossing which, brought us to the Three Rivers, where we halted the second night. The river at this place takes a serpentine course, which compels you to ford it three times in one mile, whence its appellation originates. Noorai [Neurea], or the Ten Mile River, is at present the only stock establishment maintained, and this will be discontinued at an early period. The whole range of country in this direction does not afford such another valuable spot as Noorai, possessing advantages over even the Happy Valley, an abundance of serviceable timber, which Wellington is destitute of.

It is more likely however that Caroline felt nothing but fear and trepidation. She and James probably walked the whole way and on reaching Summer Hill military post where two privates of the 17th Regt of foot were stationed were probably stopped and questioned. James may have been asked to show his ticket of leave to prove he was allowed to be in the area.

Figure 20: Fording the Bell River[145]

[145] Watson, W.L., and Col. Mundy. 1852. *Fording the Bell River [Picture] / on Stone by W.L. Walton, from a Sketch by Col. Mundy.* 1 print : lithograph ; 11 x 18.2 cm. National Library of Australia.

James may also have introduced Caroline to his old mate John Williams who was living in the area. They had shared many hardships at both the Wellington Valley convict settlement and on Sturt's journey and John had landed himself an excellent job working as William Lane's overseer[146] on his Frederick's Valley property, where he had the run of things. The Lane's were busy building their home back near Bathurst and relied on John to manage everything in their absence.

It was an isolated job, and he must have enjoyed catching up. He would have brought them food like "hung beef and some vegetables"[147] and bread just like he had done when the missionaries had passed through a few months before. He may also have travelled part of the way with them catching up on more news or simply for company.

Leaving Summer Hill, they soon came to Broken Shaft Creek, named "on account of the many shafts that have been broken there."[148] Crossing the creek they then travelled along the rugged road to James' home near Neurea.

There were no shops, no neighbours, no support, no services, it really was a frontier, and it was a frontier with no other white women that Caroline could see.

Figure 21: Molong 1825-1828[149]

On reaching her new home Caroline was given the domestic tasks to do, like laundering and needlework.[150] She helped produce food supplies and was forced to live as James' wife. She had to do whatever it took to survive. Her survival was also threatened by disease and potential violence from bushrangers, who continued in the area.

---

[146] 'The Wellington Valley Project,' Watson's Journal.

[147] Ibid.

[148] 'The Wellington Valley Project,' Handt's Journal.

[149] Earle, Augustus. n.d. *Moolong Plains, near Wellington Valley. N.S.Wales*. Mitchell Library, State Library of New South Wales. Accessed 6 April 2022. https://collection.sl.nsw.gov.au/record/16AJjPon/Gyg5w4mmzML8o.

[150] Wiblin. 44.

Following the massacres of the Wiradyuri people around Bathurst they were displaced and recorded as "camping on properties of pastoralists who were a little bit more sympathetic."[151] Around Wellington Valley the encroachment by the settlers was in its infancy and the impact on Wiradjuri less. It seems plausible that because James had survived in the area for so many years that he had an amicable relationship with the Wiradyuri people. His isolation would have made him an easy target for retaliation if he hadn't.

Caroline would have been acutely aware that whilst James offered her protection, he was also her biggest threat and she fell pregnant soon after her arrival.

In the remote wilderness, Caroline gave birth to her son, Samuel.[152] Alone with James as her only support.

Her maternal instincts took over as she navigated the trials of new motherhood. Becoming a mother also fortified her will to survive, a survival that was always threatened by disease and potential violence.

Figure 22: Woman Outside a Bark Hut[153]

[151] Bennett, Michael quoted in *ABC News*. 17 Aug 2018. 'How the Wiradyuri Survived First Contact with European Settlers'. Accessed 2 July 2024. https://www.abc.net.au/news/2018-08-17/curious-central-west-how-the-Wiradyuri-survived-first-contact/10128822.

[152] How long Caroline remained in Mrs Black's service is uncertain. The first official record we have of Caroline after leaving the Female Factory is an application to marry on the 31st of January 1835, however it is possible that she left well before this date. From a sparsity of records, it has been deduced that Caroline gave birth to a son named Samuel Dover as early as 1833. Samuel's age at death was 83 in 1915 putting his birth as 1832, however, given that there is no mention of Caroline giving birth on the ship, it seems reasonable to assume there is an error in the informant's knowledge. There are no baptismal records for Samuel. Death source: GeniCert, trans. 2022. 'Transcript of New South Wales Death Certificate #1915/16610 for Samuel Dover'.

[153] American & Australasian Photographic Company. 1870. *Woman Outside Bark Hut House, Gulgong*. Mitchell Library, State Library of New South Wales. Accessed 28 April 2022. https://collection.sl.nsw.gov.au/record/Yr86Vybn.

Needing supplies, they returned to Bathurst in January 1835. On the 31st of that month, James sought the counsel of Rev. J.E. Keane, local minister, and applied for permission to wed Caroline. He was thirty-eight and she was just nineteen. Convicts like Caroline, under sentence, and those, like James, who held a ticket of leave, were compelled to seek approval for marriage. In most cases it was the man who applied.[154] Permission was granted almost a month later on the 26th of February long after they had returned home to the Wellington Valley. They were never married.[155]

By August 1835, the country had been in drought for months. One report stated that "rain has been so long a stranger there that the country is literally bare of grass, and great numbers of sheep are daily dying of want."[156]

The stock losses were devastating. Most people were employed in the animal trade and were impacted. James, however, was not. He was selling sly grog.

On the 7th of April 1837 Caroline gave birth to a second son who was baptised as James Dober[157] by the newly arrived missionary at Wellington Valley, Reverend James Günther. The holy man happened to be travelling through the area ministering to anyone he met. Caroline must have been ecstatic when he turned up even though she was not religious. He remarked in 1836 that:

> *it is with heartfelt satisfaction that the missionaries can record the fact that when they entered the huts of Europeans, far in the bush, with the Bible in their hands and the word of christian counsel on their lips, rarely, very rarely has it occurred that they have not met with a cordial welcome and received thanks for their kindness and pious admonitions. And there is reason to hope that more than one wandering sheep has thus been reclaimed and restored to the fold of Jesus Christ.*[158]

The wandering sheep that were James and Caroline were not reclaimed. Just two months later James was arrested and fined £30 for "retailing spirits without a licence."[159] A not insignificant amount when compared to a squatting licence which cost £10 and was considered a "large sum."[160] Even a £5 fine was a "crushing punishment… [that could] ruin him entirely."[161]Most fines issued by the courts at this time generally came with the caveat that if the person could not pay, they would be imprisoned. Stated in terms of; fined 20shillings, in default of payment to be imprisoned for 14 days. The size of the fine had a corresponding time in prison and could include other punishments. No records of James being imprisoned have been found.

---

[154] 'Permission To Marry.' 2022. Female Convicts Research Centre Inc. Accessed 10 April 2022. https://www.femaleconvicts.org.au/administration/ptom.

[155] If Caroline was a consenting party, then they would have had to travel back to Bathurst and wait for at least three weeks for the Banns to be published. It is likely that Caroline did not consent to getting married.

[156] Sydney Gazette and New South Wales Advertiser. 1835. 'EXTRAORDINARY PROSECUTION.', 1 August 1835. National Library of Australia. 2. http://nla.gov.au/nla.news-article2199505.

[157] 'Registers of Baptisms, Burials and Marriages, Series NRS 12937, Reel 5005, Baptism James Dober, V18371504 22'. 1837. Museums of History NSW - State Archives Collection.

[158] 'Wellington Valley Project,' Watson's Reports, iii 1836

[159] *Sydney Monitor (NSW:1828-1838)*. 1837. 'Bathurst.', 31 July 1837. National Library of Australia. 2. http://nla.gov.au/nla.news-article32156820.

[160] Ibid.

[161] *Sydney Monitor*. 1837. 'SCANDALOUS OUTRAGE.', 8 May 1837. National Library of Australia. National Library of Australia. 4. http://nla.gov.au/nla.news-article32155912.

James' fine was catastrophic, and he disappeared from all records. He was granted his conditional pardon on the 1st of November 1837[162] but he never picked it up. The document that granted him his freedom was still sitting in the Principal Superintendent of Convicts Office in Sydney on the 18th of February 1839 waiting for collection with "payment of the Fees due."[163]

The logical explanation for his disappearance was death. Living at Neurea away from a minister or an undertaker, his death would have been unrecorded, and his body buried where he died.[164]

---

[162]*New South Wales Government Gazette*. 1837. 'PARDONS.', 1 November 1837. National Library of Australia. 821. http://nla.gov.au/nla.news-article230670940.

[163] *New South Wales Government Gazette*. 1839. 'Government Gazette Notices', 20 February 1839. National Library of Australia. 236. http://nla.gov.au/nla.news-article230382935.

[164] Another possibility was the burial record for a James Donner on the 2nd of May 1841 which was found in Sydney. The age [37] matches James. His abode was the General Hospital with the burial taking place at St James' Parish. See 'Registers of Baptisms, Burials and Marriages, Series NRS 12937, Reel 5006, Burial James Donner V1841282 25B'. 1841. Museums of History NSW - State Archives Collection.

If this was James Dauber then the question is raised as to why he never picked up his conditional pardon in the four years since it was granted. It seems more likely that he died out in the bush.

CHAPTER 6
CAROLINE AND JOHN

Following the baptism of baby James Dober in 1837, Caroline is not mentioned again in any records until the May 5th, 1846, when she appeared in Bathurst at the baptism of her two latest children, John and Sarah Williams. She had avoided being mentioned in any correspondence, not even when her seven years of servitude had finished. Her re-emergence at the baptism shows the father was John Williams.[165]

The two new additions were John born on the 18th of July 1841,[166] and Sarah born on the 29th of September 1844.[167] John was working as a labourer, and the family was living on the Lachlan River. These few basic facts provide a glimpse into what Caroline had been doing and where she had been.

James Dauber's death not only left Caroline feeling vulnerable to attack and exploitation from her isolation, but it also made her desperate to protect her two young boys. She had few options and few acquaintances.

The timing was critical because if James had died before her seven-year sentence was completed, she would have been sent back to the authorities for redistribution and if she was still breastfeeding, Caroline knew she would likely be sent back to the factory and her old mistress, Mrs. Black.[168] It would not have been a bad option to put a roof over their heads, food in their bellies, and offer protection. Given that the government was fastidious with their record-keeping of convicts and that no records have been found, it seems logical to conclude that Caroline was already a free woman when James died, leaving her free to choose her path.

She had gained her freedom on the 18th of October 1838 and son John Williams was conceived at the end of 1840. The logical conclusion must be that James died between these dates and the new relationship with John Williams began.

John had been convicted in the Kent assizes court and sentenced to be transported for life. The assizes court was presided over by a judge as opposed to the justice of the peace that heard Caroline's case. He heard more serious cases.

He arrived on the *Minerva I (4)* in 1824. On arrival, he had been sent straight to Wellington Valley, where he was employed as a labourer. Having obtained his ticket of leave for his part in Sturt's expedition, the thirty-seven-year-old had been required to stay in the area. He had found work with William Lane and was carving out his

---

165 *Author's Note:* Over one hundred and ninety men with the name John Williams have been researched to try and find Caroline's partner. Of the convicts all can be ruled out as a match except John of the Minerva I (4).[165] There were also eight John Williams born in the colony up to 1823[165] who cannot be ruled out as Caroline's partner.

166 'Registers of Baptisms, Burials and Marriages, Series NRS 12937, Reel 5009, Baptism John W Williams, V18411933 31A'. 1841. Museums of History NSW - State Archives Collection.

167 'Registers of Baptisms, Burials and Marriages, Series NRS 12937, Reel 5009, Baptism Sarah Williams, V18441934 31A'. 1844. Museums of History NSW - State Archives Collection.

168 Frost, Lucy. 2006. 'Female Factories'. The Companion to Tasmanian History. 2006. https://www.utas.edu.au/library/companion_to_tasmanian_history/F/Female%20factories.htm.

own life. He had never married so when the opportunity to look after Caroline and her boys arose, he appears to have been more than willing to gain an instant family.

John received his conditional pardon towards the end of 1837[169] and was able to move anywhere in the colony. An opportunity arose for him on the Lachlan River, which he took up. The Lachlan River formed the southern boundary of the Carcoar Police District from its junction with the Crookwell River to its junction with the Belubula River. By October 1840 labourers and shepherds were in such shortage in the area that they could earn "exorbitant wages."[170] John who had experience as an overseer and labourer would have been highly regarded.

The family lived in relative obscurity. The Lachlan River area was another frontier and just as remote as Wellington Valley had been. Caroline undertook the domestic chores and would have worked around the home and garden. Even though "the demand for female labour was so strong"[171]it is unlikely that she would have undertaken additional paid work.

The remote location meant that after the birth of John and Sarah no minister was on hand and no church nearby so no baptism could not be immediately performed.

After years at their remote home, the day came for a trip to Bathurst. It was a big undertaking, packing up the children and supplies for the journey. They must all have been so excited, no more so than the pregnant Caroline, who had planned for all the necessities she had to buy and wondered at the changes she would see and the news she could hear.

It was 1846 and John had decided that their two children would be baptised. The church hadn't played a substantial role in Caroline's life, and she was indifferent to the decision to have John aged four and Sarah aged twenty months baptised. She went along with John's wishes, however her thirteen-year-old son, Samuel Dauber, remained unbaptised.

The family returned to their home laden with supplies. Caroline could now sew new clothes with the fabrics she had bought, and she could pass on news to her distant neighbours.

Towards the end of the year, she gave birth to her fourth son, William.[172] He was never baptised, an indication that John had disappeared from Caroline's life. No further records of John exist after the 1846 Bathurst baptisms, so in all probability he died in the remote Lachlan River area leaving Caroline to bury another partner in the paddock of her home.

---

[169] New South Wales Government Gazette. 1837. 'PARDONS.', 821.

[170] *Sydney Herald*. 1840. 'LACHLAN RIVER.', 16 October 1840. National Library of Australia. 3. http://nla.gov.au/nla.news-article12866064.

[171] Wiblin, Sue, 44.

[172] Murrin, Joy, trans. 2009. 'Transcript of New South Wales Death Certificate #1917/15873 for William Williams', lists his place of birth as Emu Swamp,[172] near present day Orange. This location may not be accurate as it relied on the informant's knowledge. William lived most of his life at Emu Swamp, so it is possible that the birth was assumed to be at the same place. There is no record of a birth or baptism for William to confirm this. Mother listed as Caroline Field.

Figure 23: Sheep Station on the Lachlan River[173]

Finding herself as a single mother again, in another remote outpost, she at least had Samuel, who was aged fifteen, and could help her. With no time to grieve she immediately set about starting again and by August 1848[174] she had started a relationship with George Conroy.

[173] Stock, Edward. 1850. *Sheep Station on the Lachlan River, (Messers Philps & Chadwick)*. Drawing. Accessed 1 May 2022. http://handle.slv.vic.gov.au/10381/56769.

[174] Date of conception of daughter Elizabeth Conroy calculated from: GeniCert, trans. 2022. 'Transcript of New South Wales Death Certificate #1925/8040 for Elizabeth Dunn'. Lists Age 76 on the 24 May 1925.

CHAPTER 7
CAROLINE AND GEORGE

George Conroy was a shepherd, a solitary occupation that required him to watch over his flock of sheep from dawn to dusk. In colonial Australia, there were no fences, so shepherds were employed in vast numbers to protect flocks of sheep. In 1846, official numbers reported there were 13,565 shepherds in New South Wales.[175]

At sunrise, he would relieve the hutkeeper or watchman from his overnight watch. He would open the hurdles which were a movable, light, cheap, and easily made yarding system, and lead the sheep to pasture, water, and shade.

Figure 24: Sheep Hurdle[176]

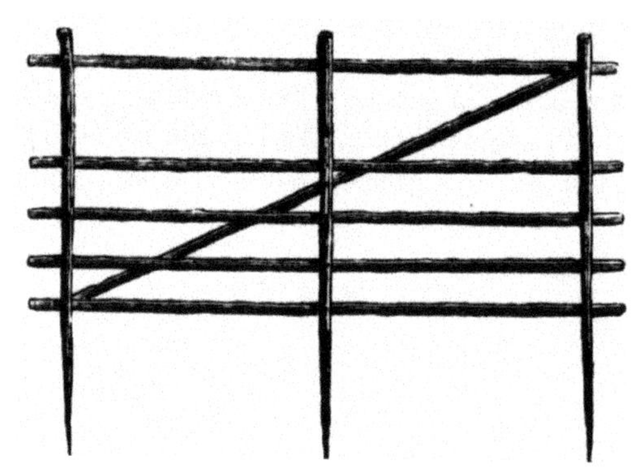

The flock size that George looked after would typically have been upwards of four hundred sheep. During summer, he would have needed to travel extensively looking for suitable feed and water. The biggest risk posed to sheep at the time, however, was attacks from dingoes and George would have been on the lookout for any animals straying. His only company was his dog who he had trained to guard the sheep.

---

[175] Southey, Thomas. 1848. The Rise, Progress and Present State of Colonial Wools: With Some Account of the Goat's Wool and Angora and India. Smith, Elder, p97

[176] *Illustrated Sydney News*. 1872. 'Sheep Hurdles', 20 February 1872. National Library of Australia. 14. http://nla.gov.au/nla.news-article63618536.

Figure 25: Shepherd 1849[177]

Figure 26: Sheep Station[178]

[177] Gill, Samuel Thomas. 1849. *Shepherd, So. [i.e. South] Australia, Adelaide, Jany 1849*. National Library of Australia. Accessed 5 May 2022. https://nla.gov.au/nla.obj-134370033.

[178] Gill, Samuel Thomas. 1855. *Out Sheep Station*. National Library of Australia. Accessed 5 May 2022. https://nla.gov.au/nla.obj-2821263488.

George can be pictured with a:

bronzed and weather beaten face, long and straggly locks and unkempt beard...His hat...an old cabbage tree, well-seasoned and holey with a red sweat-stained handkerchief around his neck. Crimean shirt, with open breast, waistcoat maybe, and lever watch. Moleskin trousers and blucher boots, with toe rags inside to take the place of socks...His coat when he wore one, [was] probably the old pea-jacket of the times, or an oilskin. His tucker slung over his shoulder, or on to his belt, were his billy, with tea and sugar for his mid-day meal of damper and salt meat, and sometimes brownie. Hardy, strong, patient and persistent.[179]

At the end of the day George drove the sheep back home and put them into the hurdles where he left them back in the charge of the hutkeeper, for the night. As George slept in the hut, the hutkeeper occupied a watch-box which was a small house with handles at each side, that could be picked up and moved. The hutkeeper had his own dog and often had a fire going to help ward of predators.

Figure 27: Hut keeper in Watchbox[180]

Both the hutkeeper and shepherd were liable for the cost of any sheep lost on their respective watches. So, they would count the sheep at the start of a shift to ensure no losses were put on them.

George's wage included food rations of ten and a half pounds of meat, ten and a half pounds of flour, seven ounces of sugar, three and a half ounces of soap and two

---

[179] Gennys, R. H. 1925. 'Shepherds and Shepherding in Australia.' *The Royal Australian Historical Society*, Part 5, 11: 281–88. National Library of Australia. https://nla.gov.au/nla.obj-594390116.

[180] Apfel, Lisa. 2023. 'Digital Photograph of 26a. [Shepherd on Bush Property]'. In *Item 02: Sketchbook of Andrew Bonar [1854, ca. 1857-1860, 1913]*. Vol. 2.

ounces of salt per week. The flour was always made into damper and cooked in the hot ashes of the fire.

Figure 28: Dingoes of the Bush Prowling Round the Sheep with watch-box and hut [181]

[181] Gill, Samuel Thomas. n.d. 'F9 Prospecting at an out Station. Dingoes, or Wild Dogs of the Bush Prowling Round the Sheep Fold.' In *Dr Doyle's Sketch Book*. Accessed 7 May 2022. https://collection.sl.nsw.gov.au/record/nQR2plX1.

Every shepherd had an annual break from his work, and most were notorious for their annual binge drinking sprees where they headed straight for the nearest hotel or sly-grog shop armed with their annual wages. While the settlers who employed the shepherds complained about the hotel keepers preying on drunken men, they were also the beneficiaries because the now penniless shepherds had no option but to return for another year of monotony.[182]

Shepherds' wages started increasing in the late 1830s because convict transportation was ending, and pastoralists had to start hiring free men. The wages then fell abruptly in the early 1840s with what was the worst depression in Australia's history. They then varied up and down until the discovery of gold in the 1850's when they soared, as all class of workers, including shepherds made their way to the goldfields.

How or where Caroline met George is unrecorded. He may have been shepherding in the Lachlan, or Caroline may have met him in town after packing up the children and heading back to town and civilization. They had however met up by 1849, because Caroline gave birth to little Elizabeth Conroy sometime towards the end of 1849 to early 1850.[183] There is no record of her birth or baptism which indicates that the family were living in a remote location again, managing the sheep flock.

George's outlook on life improved with an instant family. Not only did he have companionship, but his employer was obliged to increase both the wages and the rations he was entitled to. Female partners of shepherds were known to take over the role of hutkeeper and children were also tasked with looking after the sheep. As a single shepherd in 1849 George could expect an annual wage of £18, however with a wife acting as hut keeper and moving the hurdles they would earn between £25 and £28 per annum.[184]

As one commentator noted in 1845:

> *A shepherd's wife must sweep the sheep-yards or remove the hurdles, in the day-time, attend to her children, and, of course, the necessary comforts of her husband. In consideration of her services, the settlers promise, ... two weekly rations for herself and children.*[185]

Whilst another noted in 1849:

> *The wife ... would be able to do watchman's duty in shifting hurdles. A married shepherd would soon be able to make his children useful in looking after his flock, while he was busy in other pursuits— boot-making or gardening.*[186]

Sixteen-year-old Samuel was the perfect age to undertake shepherding tasks and would have been put to work immediately. James was twelve and capable of

---

[182] Pickard, John. 2008. 'Shepherding in Colonial Australia'. *Rural History* 19 (1): 55–80. https://doi.org/10.1017/S0956793307002300.

[183] GeniCert, trans. 2022. 'Transcript of New South Wales Death Certificate #1925/8040 for Elizabeth Dunn'. States age at death as 76 in 1925 and aged at marriage as 18 in 1869.

[184] *Geelong Advertiser*. 1849. 'GEELONG MARKETS.', 14 April 1849. National Library of Australia. 1. http://nla.gov.au/nla.news-article93139106.

[185] *The Australian*. 1845. 'To the Editor of the Australian.', 23 October 1845. National Library of Australia. 4. http://nla.gov.au/nla.news-article37155747.

[186] *South Australian Gazette and Mining Journal*. 1849. 'LIFE IN THE BUSH —THE SHEPHERD.', 17 February 1849. National Library of Australia. 4. http://nla.gov.au/nla.news-article195937150.

undertaking many tasks. As he and then eight-year-old John and three-year-old William got older their chores progressively increased. All the boys continued with rural occupations later in their lives including carrier, drover, labourer and farmer. Samuel and James began being referred to as Dover instead of Dauber in official records.[187][188][189][190][191]

With more hands available George and Caroline could supplement their diet by growing vegetables and hunting wildlife for meat, they may even have been able to purchase a cow for milk and chickens for eggs.

In 1851 they heard whispers that gold had been discovered nearby by a couple of local boys including William Lane's nephew. They could never have foreseen the rush that was about to hit when the newspapers broke the story of Australia's first payable gold discovery in May. Ophir was the destination of the hoards, and the roads were soon filled with travellers. George however was not swept up with the mania, choosing to continue shepherding. Perhaps he realised that with a shortage of workers he was in a great bargaining position for a pay rise.

Figure 29: Bathurst 1851[192]

[187] Middleton, Alex, and Francis Beresford Maning. 1886. *Bathurst and Western District Directory and Tourist's Guide and Gazetteer*. Bathurst: J. Virtue & Company. 55.

[188] GeniCert, trans. 2022. 'Transcript of New South Wales Death Certificate #1915/16610 for Samuel Dover'.

[189] GeniCert, trans. 2021. 'Transcript of New South Wales Marriage Certificate #1860/2278 for James Dover and Eliza Dunn'.

[190] GeniCert, trans. 2022. 'Transcript of New South Wales Death Certificate #1856/2706 for George Conroy

[191] GeniCert, trans. 2021. 'Transcript of New South Wales Death Certificate #1902/7447 for James Dover'.

[192] Angas, George French. 1851. *Bathurst*. Accessed 1 May 2022. http://handle.slv.vic.gov.au/10381/136967.

By 1853 the family were living close to Orange. The town was booming, being the closest town to Ophir. But for Catholics like George, they didn't have a resident priest who could minister to them. Father Bernard Murphy would however visit from Carcoar at various times, and so it was in April, he came to Orange. George wasted no time in getting their newest addition, one month old Caroline baptised.[193]The shift from her own protestant upbringing to a catholic baptism for her daughter again shows Caroline's apathy for religion. She simply didn't care about the issue and went along with George's wishes.

George started to feel unwell in February 1855. After a visit with the local doctor, he was diagnosed with cancer. The devastating news was compounded for Caroline who was seven months pregnant at the time.

George although feeling ill had set his family up at Emu Swamp. It was a little area near the thriving and close-knit Cornish Settlement[194], which was made up of devout Wesleyan Methodist settlers, predominantly from Cornwall. The settlers here, like elsewhere were in need of reliable workers and George with stepsons Samuel, James, John and William were welcomed as valuable additions.

It is probable that Caroline would have been welcomed on mentioning her second "husband" John Williams. This was the area she had first met him, and now many of William Lane's family, including a sister Ann, lived in or near the Cornish Settlement.

Caroline must have appreciated having women close by who could support her when she gave birth in April to her latest son Henry. The little baby was baptised just like his sister Caroline when Father Murphy made a trip to Orange on a freezing June morning.

George was asked by the Wesleyan lay preacher William Tom (husband of Ann Lane) to contribute to The Patriotic Fund, which was raising funds to aid the fight in the Crimean War.[195]Although having little to spare, George realised the importance of being valued in this community. His time was running out and he wanted his family supported after his death, so he gave five shillings.

On the 18th of November 1856, George lost his battle with cancer. The date is significant because from the 1st of March that year all deaths had been required by law to be registered.[196] Nineteen-year-old James complied by registering his stepfather's death at the Orange Court House. Caroline was not the informant, and no further records of her have been found. Since no record of her death has ever been found it seems that she must have died between the birth of son Henry in April 1855 and the introduction of compulsory registration on the 1st of March 1856. When examining later marriage and death certificates for her children a compelling argument for her dying in this period can be mounted. Caroline's name is remembered on Samuel's death certificate and John's first marriage certificate.

---

[193] 'Registers of Baptisms, Burials and Marriages, Series NRS 12937, Reel 5026, Baptism Caroline Conroy, V1852822 70'. 1841. Museums of History NSW - State Archives Collection.

[194] Now known as Byng

[195] *Bathurst Free Press and Mining Journal*. 1855. 'Advertising', 7 July 1855. National Library of Australia. 3. http://nla.gov.au/nla.news-article62054300.

[196] 'Registry Records.' n.d. NSW Registry of Births Deaths & Marriages. NSW Government. Accessed 13 October 2023. https://www.nsw.gov.au/family-and-relationships/family-history-search/registry-records.

William knew her name was Caroline but did not know her surname. None of the younger children have her name listed on their marriages or deaths indicating that neither they nor the informants of their deaths remembered her details.

No burial record has been found for her either. This is not surprising when we discover that cemeteries exist in the area with unknown graves. They were managed by private individuals as trustees and the private records have not survived.[197]

With the deaths of both Caroline and George, it fell to the older boys to raise their siblings including baby Henry. A feat that they somehow managed.

Samuel never married but lived in the Emu Swamp area until the ripe old age of eighty-three.[198] James went on to marry Eliza Dunn in February 1860[199] and to have seventeen children. He died aged sixty-five in May 1902 at Wellington[200] back near his birthplace. John remained at Emu Swamp and was married twice[201][202] with fifteen children from both marriages. He died in 1903 aged sixty-two.[203] Sarah married John Manning and had eight children before dying at only forty-seven in Orange. William remained at Emu Swamp and had nine children by his first two wives[204]. He had no issue with his third wife before passing away aged seventy-one in 1917[205]. Elizabeth married John Dunne[206] and had ten children before dying in 1925 in Orange.[207] Caroline married William House at Emu Swamp in 1874[208] and had six children in Orange. Henry married Malvina Johnson in Molong[209] and had eleven children. He died in 1935 aged eighty at Yeoval.[210]

---

197 Howarth, Jennifer. 2023. 'A History of the Burials in Lewis Ponds Cemetery 1861-1919'. Submitted in Partial Fulfilment of the Diploma of Family Historical Studies of the Society of Australian Genealogists.

198 GeniCert, trans. 2022. 'Transcript of New South Wales Death Certificate #1915/16610 for Samuel Dover'.

199 GeniCert, trans. 2021. 'Transcript of New South Wales Marriage Certificate #1860/2278 for James Dover and Eliza Dunn'.

200 GeniCert, trans. 2021. 'Transcript of New South Wales Death Certificate #1902/7447 for James Dover'.

201 Turtle, Laurence, trans. 2008. 'Transcript of New South Wales Marriage Certificate #1860/2273 for John Williams.

202 Turtle, Laurence, trans. 2008. 'Transcript of New South Wales Marriage Certificate #1878/4326 for John Williams and Sarah Fardell'.

203 New South Wales Births, Deaths and Marriages. 2019. 'Death Certificate #3086/1903 for John Williams'.

204 Murrin, Joy, trans. 2009. 'Transcript of New South Wales Marriage Certificate #1871/3116 for William Williams and Sarah Ann Smalley'.

205 Murrin, Joy, trans. 2009. 'Transcript of New South Wales Death Certificate #1917/15873 for William Williams'.

206 GeniCert, trans. 2022. 'Transcript of New South Wales Marriage Certificate #1869/3091 for John Dunne and Elizabeth Conroy'.

207 GeniCert, trans. 2022. 'Transcript of New South Wales Death Certificate #1925/8040 for Elizabeth Dunn'.

208 GeniCert, trans. 2023. 'Transcript of New South Wales Marriage Certificate #1874/3466 for William House and Caroline Conroy'.

209 GeniCert, trans. 2023. 'Transcript of New South Wales Marriage Certificate #1881/4701 for Henry Cornroy (sic) and Malvina Jane Johnson'.

210 GeniCert, trans. 2023. 'Transcript of New South Wales Death Certificate #1935/6966 for Henry Conroy'.

EPILOGUE

SARAH FIELD

As Caroline set sail for Australia in 1832 her family in Birmingham were also changing location. They moved to the heart of the city, to Ann Street, Court 5, house 8. It was a back-to-back house that had been constructed to try and ease the overcrowding that Birmingham was experiencing. These houses were simply built back-to-back, meaning there was one entrance on the front and a common rear wall shared with their neighbour's home; They were two or three storeys high with one room at each level. The ground floor was the living area including the kitchen and the higher levels were the bedroom/s. All the houses were arranged around a central court or yard where the communal laundry, lavatory and tap were located. Access to the yard was through a shared walkway from the street.

Figure 30: Back-to-Back Plan

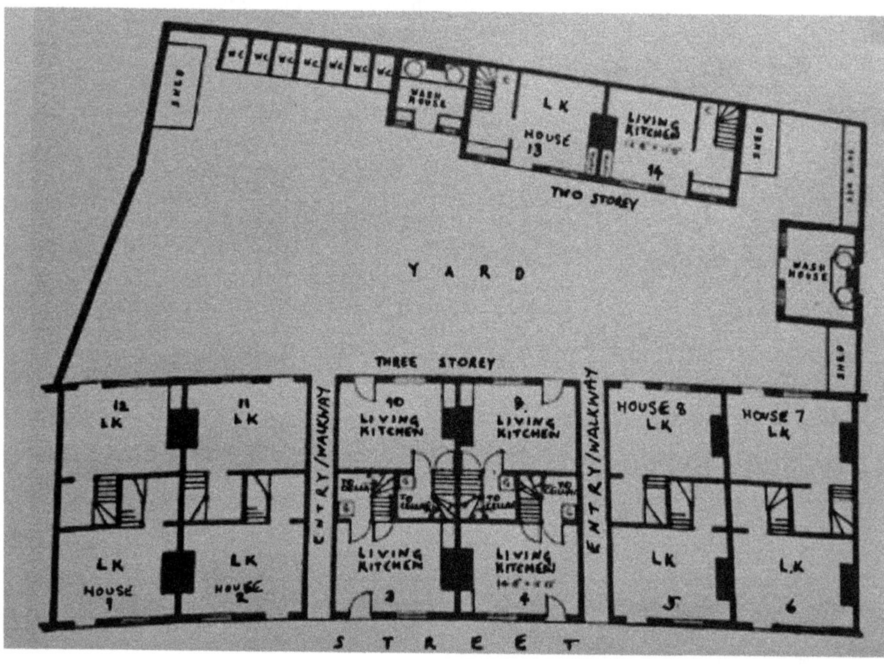

Court 5 was in a state of disrepair and had poor drainage.[211] This combined with its unpaved surface ensured the yard was always a quagmire after rain.

When Sarah and husband, William Horton, first moved in the four boys, Joseph, Samuel, John and Fred would have slept top to toe in one bed. Their bed would have been on the third storey alongside any work area that William had. Two-year-old Harriet, being the only girl, would have had her own bed.

Sarah had her final child, Edwin Horton in 1837, five years after Caroline reached Australian shores. As the family grew, they continued living in the same house with twenty-one-year-old Joseph still there in 1841.[212]

Harriet grew and was responsible for helping Sarah with all the household chores. At seven her jobs included emptying the chamber pots every morning. Carrying them downstairs, she was careful not to spill the contents. Entering the yard she then emptied them into the miskin [large bin] ready for collection by the miskin man [sewerage collection man].

With a common yard and shared facilities, it was necessary for the residents to plan and roster washing days. In 1841 there were forty-nine people living in the ten houses that made up court 5. Living with the shared space meant neighbours knew each other well. Each formed opinions of the others and in Sarah case, she thought that the King family were untrustworthy, saying "neither she nor any of the neighbours would trust their children to the[ir] care."[213] Her opinion was voiced in the inquest into Elizabeth King's infant daughter's death. Sarah was a key witness.

It transpired that eighteen-year-old Elizabeth or Betsy as she was known, had thrown her infant daughter into the Worcester Canal where she drowned. Sarah testified that:

> *She had known the prisoner twelve or thirteen years. On Saturday week the prisoner came to her house after leaving the Workhouse [where she had been for a month after giving birth]. She (Mrs H.) gave her some bread to feed the infant, and another neighbour gave her sugar, and she made the victuals [food]. At dinner time she (Mrs H.) nursed the child for the prisoner, and her sister came and nursed it for a short time...At half-past three o'clock on Saturday afternoon the prisoner was leaving the house with the child, when she (Mrs H.)told her to wrap it warm and went away to Mr White's, the relieving officer.*[214]

---

[211] Coles-Harris, Jenni. n.d. 'A Tour of Lost Birmingham: Street by Street: A Short History of Ann Street.' *A Tour of Lost Birmingham* (blog). Accessed 29 March 2022. Image 10. https://mappingbirmingham.blogspot.com/2012/01/short-history-of-ann-street.html.

[212] '1841 England Census for Sarah Horton. Warwickshire, Birmingham, St Paul, District 6. Image 10'. 1841. Ancestry. Accessed 29 March 2022. https://www.ancestry.com.au.

[213] *Birmingham Journal*. 21 Oct 1843. 'Inquest.' British Newspaper Archive. Accessed 20 June 2024. https://www.britishnewspaperarchive.co.uk/.

[214] Ibid

Figure 31: Ann Street in 1823 with the back-to-backs on the right.[215]

Mr White was one of the men who distributed poor relief,[216] "in the form of vouchers or tokens which could be cashed at the workhouse."[217] The vouchers were handed in at the workhouse in exchange for food. The workhouse was the only place vulnerable people such as young unmarried mothers, the elderly and sick could turn for support. It had limited places to house people and most support was provided as outdoor relief in the form of the vouchers. In the winter of 1837 there were over three thousand people receiving outdoor relief.

Elizabeth, however, didn't go to Mr White because she needed a roof over her head. Her unemployed mother had already been to see the workhouse governor to plead her case. She had asked him to keep Elizabeth and her baby for a few more months because she couldn't support her, but he replied: "they must turn out all the bitches together."[218]

Elizabeth was distraught and depressed. Another neighbour, Maria Thompson, stated: "She seemed very sad- very down…I do not think she is as right in her head as she ought to be."[219] Maria claimed that Elizabeth told her that "she didn't know

---

[215] *The Old Hay Market, Now Ann Street, June 21, 1823, Now Colmore Row 1888*. n.d. Birmingham Museums Trust. Accessed 2 June 2024. https://dams.birminghammuseums.org.uk/asset-bank/action/viewAsset?id=7438&index=26&total=84&view=viewSearchItem.

[216] *Birmingham Gazette*. 28 Feb 1842. 'Birmingham Guardians of the Poor.' British Library Newspapers. Accessed 12 June 2024. 1.https://link.gale.com/apps/doc/EN3216072842/BNCN?sid=bookmark-BNCN&xid=de1ce709.

[217] 'A History of the County of Warwick: Vol 7, the City of Birmingham. Political and Administrative History: Local Government and Public Services.' 1964. British History Online. Accessed 13 June 2024. https://www.british-history.ac.uk/vch/warks/vol7/pp318-353#h3-s4.

[218] Birmingham Journal 21 Oct 1843

[219] Ibid

what to do"[220] because she had nowhere to go. Both her sister and the workhouse had kicked her out.

The next morning Elizabeth turned up at court 5 without the baby. It's body was fished out of the canal later that day and taken to the police station where Sarah and Maria Thompson had to identify it.

Elizabeth was arrested and a coroner's inquest was held and found that "the prisoner put the child into the water while in a state of insanity."[221] They then released her.

Sarah and William celebrated the marriage of Harriet in 1849 to Frederick Woollaston.[222] The young couple found that one of the houses in Court 5 had become available and they moved in. Sarah must have been overjoyed having Harriet right next door.

By 1851 only had Edwin remained at home. He was fourteen and attending school. As well as having Harriet as a neighbour, the Kings were also still next door. Betsy remained unmarried and at home with her sister and mother.[223]

Harriet and Frederick's family grew and by 1861 they had moved from court 5. The King family, however remained.[224]

At the ripe old age of seventy-two Sarah died on the 3rd of March 1864.[225] She had succumbed to bronchitis, no doubt the result of living with constant plumes escaping the chimneys of Birmingham.

---

[220] Ibid

[221] Ibid.

[222] 'Birmingham, England, Church of England Marriages and Banns, 1754-1939 for Harriet Horton, Birmingham, St Martin.' 1849. Ancestry. Accessed 13 June 2024. https://www.ancestry.com.au.

[223] '1851 England Census, Warwickshire, Birmingham, St Paul, 01.' 1851. Ancestry. Accessed 13 June 2024. Images 18-19. https://www.ancestry.com.au.

[224] '1861 England Census for Sarah Horton, Warwickshire, Birmingham, St Paul, District 01. Image 16'. 1841. Ancestry. Accessed 13 June 2024. https://www.ancestry.com.au.

[225] 'Death Registration: Sarah Horton 1864 Vol 6d p102'. n.d. HM Passport Office. General Register Office. Accessed 9 June 2024. www.gro.gov.uk.

SAMUEL HORTON

Caroline's fifteen-year-old half- brother Samuel spent as much time away from the cramped conditions in Ann Street as he could, returning only to sleep. Early in 1837[226] he was found guilty of steeling two brass castings from Josiah Taylor. It transpired that he had been stopped between 10pm and 11pm and searched by street keeper Thomas Hale, who was employed to keep order in the street. When Hale asked where the brass castings came from, Samuel replied that his father gave them to him. Hale arrested him and took him to the watch house. After further enquiries his employer George Robinson identified the castings as belonging to Taylor.[227] Samuel was sentenced to four days in gaol and then to be sent to the asylum.[228] The asylum was used to house juvenile offenders until they could be "discharged thoroughly reformed."[229] How long Samuel was at the asylum isn't recorded.

After his release he was again caught stealing on the 12th of August 1840. He was following in Caroline's steps and was sent to Warwick where he was tried at the county assizes and sentenced to ten years transportation.[230]The eighteen-year-old brass moulder was taken to the *Fortitude* prison hulk to await his ship to a foreign port.

Samuel's character was described as "bad in prison often."[231] After waiting for three months in the foetid hulk, he was put on board the *Lady Raffles* bound for Van Dieman's Land.

New South Wales was no longer accepting convicts. Three years earlier the free settlers had pushed for the abolition of convict transportation and the question had been debated and partially won by the anti-transportationists. Their concession to the cessation of transportation to New South Wales was that it could continue to Van Diemen's Land.

Samuel arrived in Hobart on the 17th of March 1841.[232] He was nineteen and the officials recorded that he was unable to read or write, however he had been recorded as able to read on the prison hulk register. He stated that his father William was a

---

[226]'Samuel Horton in Calendars of Prisoners, 1801-1850, in the Warwickshire Quarter Sessions Film #4415779. Image 490'. 1837. FamilySearch. Accessed 2 June 2024.
https://www.familysearch.org/search/catalog/show?availability=Family%20History%20Library.

[227] 'Samuel Horton in Depositions, 1824-1850 in the Warwickshire Quarter Sessions. Film #004415095. Images 401-402'. 1837. FamilySearch. Accessed 2 June 2024.
https://www.familysearch.org/search/catalog/show?availability=Family%20History%20Library.

[228] 'Samuel Horton in Calendars of Prisoners, 1801-1850, in the Warwickshire Quarter Sessions Film #4415779. Image 490'. 1837. FamilySearch. Accessed 2 June 2024.
https://www.familysearch.org/search/catalog/show?availability=Family%20History%20Library.

[229] *Birmingham Gazette*. 5 Nov 1827. 'BIRMINGHAM, Nov. 5, 1827'. British Library Newspapers. Accessed 10 June 2024. 3. https://link.gale.com/apps/doc/EN3216063222/BNCN?sid=bookmark-BNCN&xid=d9312db0.

[230] 'England & Wales, Criminal Registers, 1791-1892 for Samuel Horton, England, Warwickshire. Image 32.' 1840. Ancestry. Accessed 31 October 2023. https://www.ancestry.com.au.

[231] 'UK, Prison Hulk Registers and Letter Books, 1802-1849 for Samuel Horton. Fortitude Register 1837-1843, Image 102'. 1840. Ancestry. Accessed 11 November 2023. https://www.ancestry.com.au.

[232] 'Conduct Registers of Male Convicts Arriving in the Period of the Probation System, CON33-1-6, Lady Raffles, Image 146 Samuel Horton'. n.d. Libraries Tasmania. Accessed 31 October 2023. https://stors.tas.gov.au/CON33-1-6$init=CON33-1-6P146.

painter residing in Ann Street, Birmingham with his four brothers Joseph, John, Fred and Edwin and his sister Harriet.[233]Mother, Sarah, was not mentioned.

The Tasmanian authorities judicially recorded every detail of the convicts in their system, presumably to aid in identifying runaways. Samuel was no exception. The description leaves us wondering if Caroline shared any of these characteristics. He was described as five feet five inches tall with a fair complexion, a small head, and light brown hair. He was clean shaven with dark brown eyebrows and light blue eyes. His visage was "rather long" with a broad forehead, short nose and medium mouth and chin. He had a couple of tattoos. One was a woman on his right arm and the other was the letter H on his left.[234]

Samuel like all the male convicts was part of the new, Probation System which, had replaced the Assignment System. Now instead of being assigned to work for settlers when they landed, convicts first had to serve a period of probation under the strict control of the government before earning the privilege of being assigned to private settlers. It was a system introduced because the English government was trying to reign in the power of the convicts.

In a report on the state of transportation it was said that:

> *You cannot, my Lord, have an idea of the vexations, which accompany the employment of convicts, or of the vicissitudes attendant upon their assignment. Their crimes and misconduct involve the settlers in daily trouble, expense, and disappointment...there is so much peculation, so much insubordination, insolence, disobedience of lawful orders, and so much drunkenness, that reference to the magisterial authority is constant, and always attended with loss of time and expense to the settlers... in numberless instances, masters are known to submit to peculation rather than incur the additional expense of prosecuting their servants. Two hundred felons, after having been for a long time under confinement in the gaols or hulks of England, and subsequently pent up on board a transport, are placed in charge of the masters or their agents, to whom they have been assigned... the assigned servant, now relieved for the first time for some months from personal restraint, eludes the vigilance of his new master, finds his way into a public house, and the first notice the settler has of his servant, is, that he is lodged in the watch house with the loss of half his clothing, or committed to gaol for felony.*[235]

The system also required the isolation of prisoners so they could reflect on their crimes and become reformed. They were exposed to a rigorous "regime of hard labour, religious instruction and education."[236] On landing he was classified as third

---

233 'Indents of Male Convicts CON14-1-8 for Samuel Horton, Images 34-35'. n.d. Libraries Tasmania. Accessed 1 November 2023. https://stors.tas.gov.au/CON14-1-8$init=CON14-1-8P34. Note Fred is recorded as Frederick an error of assumption on the recorder's part. He was Alfred.

234 'Convict Description List CON18-1-26 for Samuel Horton'. n.d. Libraries Tasmania. Accessed 2 November 2023. https://stors.tas.gov.au/CON18-1-26$init=CON18-1-26p127.

235 'The Parliamentary Report on Transportation (1838)'. 2002. Extracts from the Molesworth Report of 1838. The Victorian Web. Accessed 20 May 2024. https://victorianweb.org/history/transpor.html.

236 Sprod, Michael. 2006. 'Probation System'. The Companion to Tasmanian History-Probation System. 2006. https://www.utas.edu.au/library/companion_to_tasmanian_history/P/Probation%20system.htm.

class, meaning he was to be sent to work on a government project. He was sent just over halfway up the east coast of Tasmania to Rocky Hills Probation Station and put to work building and maintaining roads in the area. At the end of the day, he and the other convicts walked back to the station where they were separated and isolated. After seven months of this dehumanising solitude Samuel decided to remove the partition boards surrounding his bed so that he could at least chat face to face with someone. He was caught and his period in third class extended by one month and seven days. On the 17th of July 1842, after sixteen months Samuel's time in the Probation System had expired and he was eligible for assignment to a private settler.

His "master"[237] lived at Longford and appeared to have some compassion, because when Samuel was charged with disobeying orders, his master interceded, asking the magistrate to only admonish him. After three years and nine months at Longford Samuel received his ticket of leave, enabling him to earn a wage.

He remained at Longford, where he met Mary Smith. The two convicts decided they wanted to marry and sought permission on the 2nd of January 1847.[238] The Colonial Secretary approved the application, but by the time the permission was received the couple had split up. Likely because they both got caught being absent without leave, which resulted in further punishments and separation. Samuel was sentenced to a month in the house of correction and to forfeit his wages[239] whilst Mary was sentenced to ten days hard labour.[240]

Samuel's loss of wages appears to have taught his employer a lesson, that if he charged him with being absent without leave, he wouldn't have to pay him. The colony was in an economic depression, and he had found a loophole. In March and April Samuel was subsequently charged and lost his wages.

Samuel could see the pattern and moved to the remote northwest, of Tasmania, to Circular Head. Here he had got one mark against his name for being drunk in late 1847,

Samuel liked Circular Head and the people in it, including a sixteen-year-old girl named Margaret Smedley. He proposed marriage. She was free but because Samuel was still under his sentence, permission was again sought from the authorities. The proposed marriage was approved on the 4th of April 1848.[241] A little over a month later they were wed at St Paul's church in Stanley.[242] Margaret then discovered she was pregnant and gave birth a year later.

Samuel had garnered support in the area and on the 27th of November 1849 was recorded as getting a conditional pardon, setting him free eight months earlier than his full ten-year sentence. Who recommended him as worthy of gaining his freedom early and why they recommended him is unrecorded.

---

237 'Conduct Registers of Male Convicts Arriving in the Period of the Probation System, Samuel Horton.'

238 'Registers of Applications for Permission to Marry, CON52/1/2 Page 379 for Samuel Horton and Mary Ann Smith'. 1847. Item. Libraries Tasmania. https://libraries.tas.gov.au/Record/NamesIndex/1254190.

239 Conduct Registers of Male Convicts Arriving in the Period of the Probation System, Samuel Horton'

240 'Convict Conduct Record - CON40-1-10 Image 93 Mary Ann Smith'. n.d. Libraries Tasmania. Accessed 10 November 2023. https://stors.tas.gov.au/CON40-1-10$init=CON40-1-10P93.

241 'Marriage Permission for Samuel Horton and Margaret Smedley.' 1848. Item. Libraries Tasmania. https://stors.tas.gov.au/CON52-1-2p200j2k.

242 'Marriage Registration Samuel Horton and Margaret Smedley.' 1848. Item. Libraries Tasmania. https://stors.tas.gov.au/NI/837117.

Samuel and Margaret moved fifty kilometres north to the coast, to a little place called Black River. They lived there for the remainder of their lives, raising their large family, before Samuel died on the 3rd of May 1900, aged eighty[243] His obituary speaks of him as a respected pioneer.[244]

Figure 32: Samuel Horton's Obituary

BLACK RIVER.

The funeral cortege at the burial of Mr Samuel Horton at Black River on Sunday was the largest ever seen there; from far and wide friends and relations gathered to pay their last tribute of respect to the deceased. Mrs R. Penty and the choir from Stanley journeyed out specially for the service, which was performed by Mr John Edwards. The late Mr S. Horton was a native of Birmingham, England, and was close on his 80th year at his demise. He was a colonist of 60 years' standing, and had lived at Black River for 54 years. He leaves a family of seven sons and six daughters; many of the former are well known on the N.W. Coast for their prowess in the cricket field. Mr Horton was extraordinarily active for his years, and the Saturday previous to his death drove in his load of potatoes to Stanley. In him we have lost another from the now few remaining early settlers, the pioneers and fathers of our island home.

[243] 'Wills, AD961-1-8 Will Number 2137 for Samuel Horton'. 1900. Item. Libraries Tasmania. https://libraries.tas.gov.au/Record/NamesIndex/1725052.

[244] *North Western Advocate and the Emu Bay Times*. 1900. 'BLACK RIVER.', 10 May 1900. National Library of Australia. http://nla.gov.au/nla.news-article64491343.

JOHN HORTON

Caroline's half-brother grew up and undertook the obscure occupation of a bayonet filer, presumably sharpening, to a fine point, the blades that were to be attached to the end of rifles.

His life was proceeding along a fairly typical trajectory. He had married Mary Heaton in 1846[245] and was anticipating the arrival of a baby in 1849,[246] when he made a fateful decision.

He and Mary's little back-to-back house was located opposite the canal wharf in Broad Street. In order to make the rent he took in his young brother Fred who was working as a brass chaser,[247] making decorations on brass objects. It wasn't ideal with Fred sleeping in the living area.[248] Being a back-to-back house John and Mary could only access their upstairs bedroom by walking through the living area, where Fred slept. John was struggling to find work as a bayonet filer and with the impending birth he was desperate for any work and took on a lowly paid job, sweeping the streets.[249]

As Mary's pregnancy progressed John, who was in debt,[250] became more desperate to provide for her and the baby. He hatched a plan with a couple of mates even though he was acutely aware of the risk that he was about to take, having lost two siblings to the other side of the world.

On the 30th of October 1849, a workday, he and his conspirators travelled 20km southwest to the village of Bromsgrove, where they were strangers and less likely to be recognised. After the long walk they arrived at the High Street at 6.30pm and started scouting the area. At 9pm they rendezvoused and agreed on their target, Matthew Dodd, the watchmaker.

They did some specific reconnaissance of his premises and decided to wait until Dodd fell asleep. His workshop was located above his house. With time to kill they went to Juggin's lodging house for coffee.

Just before 11pm John left for Dodd's. He climbed to the second story of the neighbouring house which enabled him to step down onto the flat gutter positioned below Dodd's workshop window. Standing on the narrow platform, which was no more than 50cm wide, with one had holding the corner for support, he smashed the window. Reaching in he started pocketing the watches. Placing them into his long coat with its torn elbow.

---

245 'Birmingham, England, Church of England Marriages and Banns, 1754-1939 for John Horton at St Philip in 1846. Image 209'. n.d. Ancestry. Accessed 15 May 2024. https://www.ancestry.com.au.

246 'Birmingham, England, Church of England Baptisms, 1813-1922 for Mary Horton at Bishop Ryder 1849. Image 36'. n.d. Ancestry. Accessed 15 May 2024. https://www.ancestry.com.au.

247 '1851 England Census for Frederick Horton in West Sheffield, Sheffield, Yorkshire, 15. Image 18.' n.d. Ancestry. Accessed 15 May 2024.

https://www.ancestry.com.au.

248 *Worcestershire Chronicle*. 1850. 'Worcestershire Lent Assizes', 13 March 1850. British Library Newspapers. 10. https://link.gale.com/apps/doc/IS3243357415/BNCN?sid=bookmark-BNCN&xid=f2693f2a. Accessed 14 May 2024.

249 Ibid

250 *Morning Post*. 1850. 'Multiple News Items', 13 March 1850. British Library Newspapers. 7. https://link.gale.com/apps/doc/R3211631380/BNCN?sid=bookmark-BNCN&xid=8e208332. Accessed 15 May 2024.

Dodd heard the window break and rushed up the stairs and into the workshop. Seeing "a man standing at the window"[251] he grabbed for him. John turned to leap up onto the neighbouring house, but Dodd caught him by his trousers. They struggled and John, desperate and full of adrenaline, kicked off with enough force to snap the buttons holding his suspenders, leaving his trousers in Dodd's hand.

Stripped of his pants John made a bee line back to Birmingham. During the evening, he had also lost his shoes and socks (if he ever had any). His plan to go unnoticed fell apart, with numerous people noticing the trouserless man wearing just a long dark coat.

Reaching Birmingham at 6am, he went straight to the horse fair where he would have been eager to sell his booty of ten watches, so that he could at least buy some new pants.

John lay low for a couple of weeks hoping to remain undetected; then on the 13 of November a warrant was issued for his arrest.[252] PC Thomas arrested him the next day and took him to the town gaol, the same goal where Caroline and Samuel had been, the same goal with The Hole and dog kennel cells. He appears to have remained here until the day of his trial, four months later. Aged twenty-five and standing just over five and a half feet tall[253], his physical description was recorded. He had:

> *Thick lips, nose very broad, thick nostrils, wide & very red, very red forehead, cut on centre of forehead, one over right eyebrow, one on under lip, dimple in chin, freckled and pock mark'd, cut on left thumb & back of left hand. Scar on right arm. Stout made.*[254]

The cuts over his forehead, his eye, his lip and his hand are a good indication that John was involved in a fight. PC Thomas made no mention that he resisted arrest, so his injuries were probably the result of a brawl. Bareknuckle fighting had been a part of the Birmingham's culture since the 1780's and "street-fights often resembled prize-fights by involving local loyalties, personal rivalries and heavy drinking."[255]His injuries combined with his conviction would have earned him the label of a 'rough.' A local term for a low-class ruffian and villain.

News of John's arrest spread at speed. Sarah must have been devastated after already seeing two of her children tried, sentenced and shipped off. She was determined not to lose John too and set about organising his defence by producing an alibi.

While John waited, he was allowed visitors and early in December he learned that Mary had given birth to a little girl. Both were doing well. Mary named the baby Mary and organised her baptism on the ninth of the same month.[256] John must have

---

[251] . *Worcestershire Chronicle*. 'Worcestershire Lent Assizes,' 13 March 1850.10

[252] 'England & Wales, Crime, Prisons & Punishments, 1770-1935 for John Horton. Series PCOM2. Source Birmingham Gaol, Warwickshire: Register of Convicts. Piece No 436'. n.d. Findmypast. Accessed 14 May 2024. https:\\findmypast.com.au.

[253] Perth DPS. n.d. 'Physical Descriptions of Convicts on the Sea Park, 1854'. Convicts to Australia. Accessed 25 May 2024. https://www.perthdps.com/.

[254] 'England & Wales, Crime, Prisons & Punishments, 1770-1935 for John Horton. Series PCOM2. Source Birmingham Gaol.'

[255] Gooderson, Philip. 2010. *The Gangs of Birmingham*. Milo Books Ltd. 41. Google-Books-ID: HOFmDwAAQBAJ

[256] 'Birmingham, England, Church of England Baptisms, 1813-1922 for Mary Horton'.

endured such emotional turmoil knowing the precarious position Mary was in, having no support.

On or about the 6th of March[257] John was taken 45km southwest to Worcester to the Worcestershire assizes. Bromsgrove is in the county of Worcestershire and so he was to face justice in that county. Also taken to Worcester at public expense were the witnesses and chief amongst the defence witnesses were Sarah and Fred.

The newspapers recorded some of the proceedings and reported that the court sat on the ninth. After the prosecution laid out their case it was Mr Richards' turn to present John's defence. He called Sarah as the first witness. She said:

> *I recollect Tuesday, the 30th of Oct., and saw the prisoner at my house on that day at half-past seven in the evening. He was working in Birmingham the following day. He swept the streets for the overseers.*[258]

On cross examination the prosecution asked her if John was at work on the 28th of October. It was a question designed to trap her in a lie because the 28th was a Sunday and men did not work on the sabbath. She replied: "Yes" and when asked would she swear it? She again said yes. The trap was sprung.

Fred was called next, and he said:

> *I saw my brother at our house on the 30th of October, and after I came home remained with him till he went to bed; he had to go through my room to his. I called him up at half-past six the next morning, and he answered me.*[259]

On cross examination he admitted that John had never stayed up until he got home from work on any other occasion and that he had never, at any other time, called out to John in the morning as he was leaving for work. It gave the impression that it was a fabricated alibi.

Justice Patterson, was aware of holes in the prosecutions' case and was clearly of the opinion that some doubt over John's guilt was evident, in his directions to the jury he said:

> *Neither mother nor brother of the prisoner had been asked if they knew the trowsers (sic) left in Mr Dodd's hands. Then again it did not appear that the prisoner had left his stockings [socks] and shoes behind him [not found at Dodd's], for though it was probable he might not have had the latter on at the time of the robbery, still there could appear no reason why he should travel without them. The witness for the prosecution, however, were positive as to the identity of the prisoner, but the jury should well consider whether it is not possible that they might have been mistaken, especially after the evidence of the prisoner's relations. However, he would leave the matter in their hands, and if there was a doubt they would assuredly give the accused the benefit of it.*

He was found guilty and sentenced to be transported for ten years.

---

[257] 'England & Wales, Criminal Registers, 1791-1892 for John Horton. England, Worcestershire, Image 5'. 1850. Ancestry. Accessed 16 May 2024. https://www.ancestry.com.au.

[258] *Worcestershire Chronicle.* 'Worcestershire Lent Assizes,' 13 March 1850.10

[259] Ibid.

Escorted out of the court he was loaded back into the prison caravan for the trip back to Birmingham town goal. He remained there until the 23rd of April 1850 when he was transferred to Millbank Prison.

Millbank was a thirty-year-old prison located next to the Thames in London. It was the largest prison in the country and was where both male and female convicts sentenced to transportation were sent to be evaluated in order to determine their final destination. John was there for six months before being transferred to Dartmoor Prison.[260]

Figure 33: Millbank Prison[261]

The probation system that Samuel had endured was being reviewed at the time of John's trial, which meant that by the time he arrived at Millbank the system had changed. The British Parliament found that the system was failing in Tasmania because there were insufficient and unsuitable buildings to house the convicts during their probation period, there were few qualified supervisors and there were too many convicts for Tasmania to support.

The Parliament said:

---

[260] 'England & Wales, Crime, Prisons & Punishments, 1770-1935 for John Horton. Series HO24. Source Millbank Prison Registers: Male Prisoners. Volume 5. Piece No 5'. n.d. Findmypast. Accessed 14 May 2024. https:\\findmypast.com.au.

[261] Frith, William Powell. 1880. *1962P1 Retribution*. Birmingham Museums Trust. Accessed 31 May 2024. https://dams.birminghammuseums.org.uk/asset-bank/action/viewAsset?id=6755&index=2&total=4&view=viewSearchItem

that any future transportation to Van Diemen's Land should not be carried on upon the old system. We thought that penal labour, previous to transportation to a distant land, should always be inflicted at home...where we could command more vigilant and careful superintendence than we could by any possibility command either in Van Diemen's Land or in Norfolk Island; where abuses could not grow up without being much more promptly discovered; and, besides, we thought that that penal labour should in all cases be preceded by separate confinement for a certain period.[262]

John was required by the new law to spend his probation period in England and was sent to Dartmoor prison to undertake his separate confinement.

Dartmoor prison was located in the southwest corner of England, in county Devon. It had been laying uninhabited since 1815 and was earmarked, in June 1850, to reopen. John was amongst the first of the 500 convicts to be taken there in October. The reason for his selection to go to Dartmoor may relate to both his skill working with metal and his age. The plan for the convicts at Dartmoor was to have them producing food as agricultural labourers.[263] They would need tools and able-bodied workers.

He was there for over three years, until the 27th of December 1853,[264] when he was transferred to the port city of Plymouth[265] where the *Sea Park* was moored. One hundred convicts from Dartmoor prison[266] were added to those already picked up at London and Portsmouth. It was bitterly cold and wet. Snow was falling so thick it settled on deck.[267] Preparations for their trip were finalised and on the first day of 1854 Captain Spedding received his instructions and set sail for Western Australia.[268]

On the 5th of April,[269] with the Western Australian Coast in sight, John and the other 303[270] convicts were given their tickets of leave. The formalities of the

---

[262] 'Convict Prisons Bill, Volume 109: Debated on Thursday 14 Mar 1850'. n.d. UK Parliament, Hansard. Accessed 20 May 2024. https://hansard.parliament.uk/Lords/1850-03-14/debates/2d7b9cd4-c746-46dd-80f9-ec23c1ec3445/ConvictPrisonsBill.

[263] *North Devon Journal*. 13 Jun 1850. 'County Intelligence.' British Library Newspapers. Accessed 20 May 2024. 8. https://link.gale.com/apps/doc/IG3225161276/BNCN?sid=bookmark-BNCN&xid=32517863.

[264] 'England & Wales, Crime, Prisons & Punishments, 1770-1935 for John Horton. Series HO8. Source Home Office: Convict Hulks, Prisons & Criminal Lunatic Asylums: Quarterly Returns of Prisoners. Piece No 118. Page 4'. n.d. Findmypast. Accessed 14 May 2024. https:\\findmypast.com.au.

[265] *Morning Chronicle (1801)*. 27 Dec 1853. 'EVENING EDITION.' British Library Newspapers. Accessed 20 May 2024. 8. https://link.gale.com/apps/doc/Y3207231311/BNCN?sid=bookmark-BNCN&xid=1794b534.

[266] *Hampshire/Portsmouth Telegraph*. 31 Dec 1853. 'FREE TRADE PROGRESS.' British Library Newspapers. Accessed 20 May 2024. 4. https://link.gale.com/apps/doc/BB3206055511/BNCN?sid=bookmark-BNCN&xid=d4f11cde.

[267] 'Sea Park, Journal of Joseph Caldwell, Surgeon, December 1853- April 1854 (File (TNA: Adm 101/253/1E)). AJCP Digitised Copy.' n.d. National Library of Australia. Accessed 20 May 2024. Image 8. https://nla.gov.au/nla.obj-2702880146.

[268] *The Standard*. 3 Jan 1854. 'Multiple News Items.' British Library Newspapers. Accessed 20 May 2024. 4. https://link.gale.com/apps/doc/R3212197548/BNCN?sid=bookmark-BNCN&xid=5c242e0b.

[269] Western Australia Convict department. 1975. '2905 John Horton. Image 107.' In *General Register of Convicts, 1848-1900 Microfilmed by the Genealogical Society of Salt Lake City. Film 918764*. Salt Lake City. Accessed 23 May 2024.

[270] *Inquirer*. 12 Apr 1854. 'SHIPPING INTELLIGENCE.' Accessed 20 May 2024. 2. http://nla.gov.au/nla.news-article65741021.

paperwork were arranged so that when they docked at Fremantle the next day the men were all available to seek employment.

On disembarking the men were divided into groups and sent to a various hiring depots[271]to prevent them inundating Fremantle.[272] At the depots they competed with new immigrants for jobs. It soon became evident that the sudden arrival of over three hundred ticket-of-leave men saturated the employment lines. The settlers had wanted convicts who could be made to work on public works and who they could use cheaply, but instead they got men still under sentence who were free to choose where they worked.[273]

The arrangement was an attempt by the British Government to wipe their hands of the cost of maintaining their convicts. They had agreed to pay for the costs associated with transporting and managing them but by landing them as ticket-of-leave holders they were effectively trying to get around the obligation of paying their upkeep. They argued that the Western Australian's should pay for them if they were sick, or unable to obtain work because they were getting the benefit of their labour.[274]

Publicly the fight was far from over with the local press stating:

> *we ought not to be liable for any expense whatever, incurred on account of ticket-of-leave or conditional-pardon men, and that the settlers will be guilty of extreme folly if they submit to any imposition of the sort. They should recollect that it is the colony which confers the favour, and not England; that without our aid the Home Government would have either to form a convict establishment in some other part of the world, at a great outlay, or keep their criminals at home...we cannot but feel perfectly certain, that they dare not, and will not, do so. They must send their convicts somewhere, and are too glad to find any colony willing to take them off their hands, and however great the expense may be, they know it is far less than if they kept the men upon English, ground.*[275]

John was granted a conditional pardon on the 10th of August 1855.[276][277]He was essentially a free man except for the condition attached banning him from returning to England. There is evidence that conditional pardons were being given as another cost saving exercise rather than a reward for good behaviour. When a ticket-of-leave

---

[271] *Perth Gazette and Independent Journal of Politics and News*. 21 Apr 1854. 'Domestic Sayings and Doings.' Accessed 20 May 2024. 2. http://nla.gov.au/nla.news-article3175162.

[272] Gibbs, Martin. 2006. 'Convict Places of Western Australia.' *Studies in Western Australian History* 24 (January):pp.71-97.

[273] *Inquirer and Commercial News*. 26 Sep 1855. 'The Inquirer & Commercial News. Quid Verum at Que Decens, Curo et Rogo, et Omnis in Hoc Sum WEDNESDAY, SEPTEMBER 26, 1855.' Accessed 21 May 2024. 2. http://nla.gov.au/nla.news-article66006584.

[274] *Inquirer and Commercial News*. 19 Sep 1855. 'PUBLIC MEETING AT PERTH.' Accessed 23 May 2024. 2. http://nla.gov.au/nla.news-article66006651.

[275] *Inquirer and Commercial News*. 1 Aug 1855. 'The Inquirer & Commercial News. WEDNESDAY, AUGUST 1, 1855.' Accessed 23 May 2024. 2. http://nla.gov.au/nla.news-article66007141.

[276] *The Western Australian Government Gazette*. 14 Aug 1855. 'Conditional Pardons.' Western Australian Legislation Website. Accessed 23 May 2024. 3. https://www.legislation.wa.gov.au/legislation/statutes.nsf/gazettes.html

[277] Western Australia Convict department. 1975. '2905 John Horton. Image 107.' In *General Register of Convicts, 1848-1900 Microfilmed by the Genealogical Society of Salt Lake City. Film 918764*. Salt Lake City. Accessed 23 May 2024.

holder was unemployed they could return to a hiring depot for food and roof over their head. The government was responsible for them as they were still under sentence. However granting a conditional pardon freed the convict but it also freed the government of the cost. The newspaper reported that they "have their pardons thrust into their hands, and whether they are willing or not the authorities oblige them to leave the depot, whether to starve or rob no one cares."[278]

No records of his whereabouts have been found. The 14th of November 1862 saw the passing of ten years since he was arrested back in Birmingham. From this point he was free to return to England if he chose.

[278] *Perth Gazette and Independent Journal of Politics and News*. 21 Sep 1855. 'THE INDEPENDENT JOURNAL.' Accessed 23 May 2024. 3. http://nla.gov.au/nla.news-article3176417.

EDWIN HORTON

On the 22nd of June 1857 Caroline's youngest half-brother also faced court. He had two prior convictions, so it would have been no surprise when he was sentenced to transportation for four years for "shopbreaking and larceny therein."[279]

The stout twenty-year-old brass cutter was described as 5 foot 3 and 1/8 inches tall with light brown hair, brown eyes, an oval face and fair complexion. His right hand was distinctively marked and scarred, and his cheekbone was also scarred.[280]Strong indications that, like John, he was also a rough.

The transportation system had again changed since John's conviction seven years before. Edwin was required to do eighteen months[281] in the Probationary System in England, before his dispatch to Australia. He was moved from Birmingham to Millbank Prison, just like John, for his evaluation. The conclusion was that he would be transferred to Pentonville Prison also in London.[282] It was built as the model prison "for carrying into effect the Separate System of discipline."[283] The separation carried through into the exercise yards and even the chapel. The only conversation Edwin had was with the guards and a minister if he chose.

On entering his 13 foot by 7-foot cell for the first time, Edwin would have been impressed with having his first glazed earthenware toilet. He also had a basin with running hot and cold water. Luxuries compared to home. His surprise, at these modern amenities would have been short lived when his cell door closed, leaving him in the dim and silent cell. The silence was created by 45cm thick brick walls, 30cm thick concrete ceiling and asphalt covered floor. Edwin had a hammock to sleep in. The isolation lasted eighteen months before he was taken to board the *Sultana* bound for Western Australia.

---

[279] 'England & Wales, Criminal Registers, 1791-1892 for Edwin Horton, Warwickshire. Image 18.' 1857. Ancestry. Accessed 10 November 2023. https://www.ancestry.com.au.

[280] 'Physical Descriptions of Convicts on the Sultana, 1859'. n.d. Convicts to Australia. https://www.perthdps.com/convicts/conwad26.htm.

[281] 'Pentonville Prison.' n.d. 19th Century Prison History. Accessed 13 November 2023. https://www.prisonhistory.org/prison/pentonville-prison-2/.

[282] 'UK, Criminal Records, 1780-1871 for Edwin Horton, Prison Registers and Statistical Returns, 1856-1857, HO 24/7, Image 221'. n.d. Ancestry. Accessed 11 November 2023. https://www.ancestry.com.au.

[283] Jebb, Joshua. 1844. *Report of the Surveyor-General of Prisons on the Construction, Ventilation, and Details of Pentonville Prison.* London: Printed by W. Clowes and sons for H.M. Stationery Office. Accessed 13 November 2023. 5. http://archive.org/details/b29300915.

Figure 34: Pentonville Prison isolated exercise yards with central guard tower[284]

Figure 35: The Chapel showing two separated prisoners in cubicles (front left)[285]

[284] Jebb. 105.

[285] *The Illustrated London News*. 1843. 'The Pentonville Prison', 7 January 1843. The Illustrated London News Historical Archive, 1842-2003. https://link.gale.com/apps/doc/HN3100005957/ILN?sid=bookmark-ILN&xid=99d37a9f.

The *Sultana* left Plymouth, on 29th of May 1859 and took 82 days to reach Fremantle arriving on the 19th of August.[286]

Edwin had less than two years to serve of his sentence.[287] He was about to turn twenty-two but was recorded as twenty-three.[288]Without having attained his ticket of leave, he was sent to Fremantle Prison to continue his Separate System of punishment.

Figure 36: The cap and silent shoes worn by Separate System convicts [289]

[286]'Australian Convict Transportation Registers – Other Fleets & Ships, 1791-1868. 1853-1863, Image 151 for Sultana 1859'. n.d. Ancestry. Accessed 13 November 2023. https://www.ancestry.com.au.

[287] 'Australian Convict Transportation Registers – Other Fleets & Ships, 1791-1868. 1853-1863, Image 158 for Edwin Horton 1859'. n.d. Ancestry. Accessed 13 November 2023. https://www.ancestry.com.au.

[288] 'Western Australia, Australia, Convict Records, 1846-1930, Convict Department, Registers (128/38-39), Image 163 for Edward Horton'. n.d. Ancestry. Accessed 14 November 2023. https://www.ancestry.com.au.

[289] Mackie, Frederick. 1853. *The Cap Worn by the Separate Treatment Prisoners*. Accessed 10 May 2024. https://nla.gov.au/nla.obj-138954202.

After four months, on the 19th of December 1859 he received his ticket of leave.[290]

His freedom was short lived. On the 23rd of July he showed that the system had not beaten him into submission, when he was charged with disobedience. A minor charge but it landed him back in Fremantle Prison for ten days.[291]

He was released and completed his sentence in June 1861.[292][293]

As a free man he struggled to stay on the straight and narrow. Having grown up in the slums and only ever known the underbelly of society he was not reformed and found himself back in court a month later. Sentenced to a month imprisonment with hard labour for receiving a stolen leather hide. The newspaper report mocked his defence implying that his lengthy speech only confirmed his guilt. It said, "The prisoner made a somewhat lengthy speech in his defence, which had the effect of removing all doubts as to his guilt."[294]

No further records of Edwin have been found. Leaving us to ponder where he went after his release. Did he meet up with John and return to England or did they both travel to parts unknown?

---

[290] 'Western Australia, Australia, Convict Records, 1846-1930, Convict Department Registers, General Register, 1850-1868 (R21b), Image 398 for Edward Horton'. n.d. Ancestry. Accessed 14 November 2023. https://www.ancestry.com.au.

[291] 'Western Australia, Australia, Convict Records…'…,' Image 163.

[292] Western Australia, Australia, Convict Records, Image 398.

[293] *The Western Australian Government Gazette*. 16 Jul 1861. 'Ticket of Leave Holders Sentence Expired.' Western Australian Legislation Website. Accessed 23 May 2024.155. https://www.legislation.wa.gov.au/legislation/statutes.nsf/gazettes.html.

[294] *Perth Gazette and Independent Journal of Politics and News*. 23. Aug 1861. 'Perth Police Court.,' 23 August 1861. National Library of Australia. 2. http://nla.gov.au/nla.news-article2933346.

APPENDIX 1

FAMILY TREE

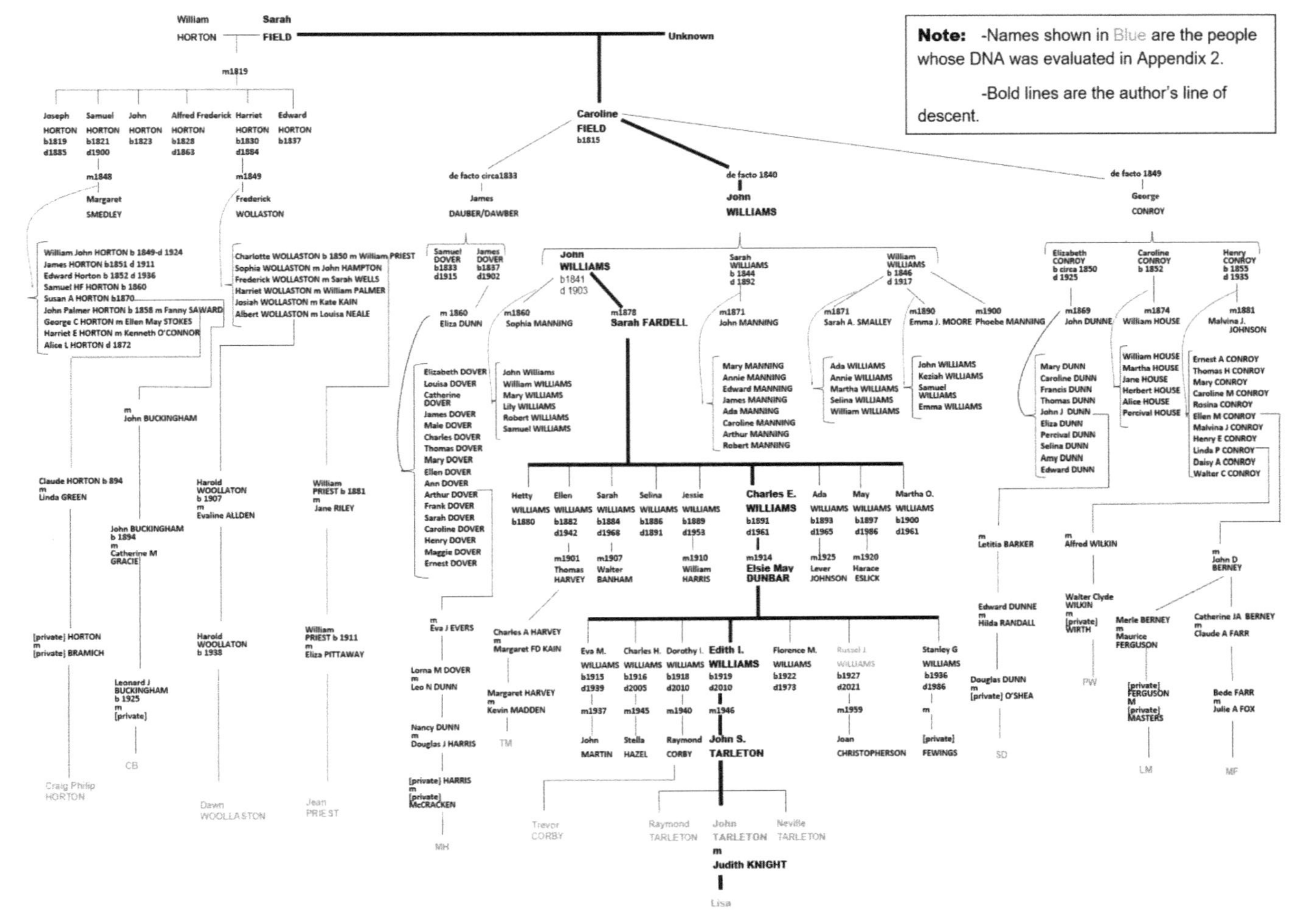

APPENDIX 2
DNA RESULTS

Caroline's convict records gave her place of conviction and her age. Working on the assumption that her birthplace may have been the same as her place of conviction I searched for possible baptism records in Birmingham. There was a match which gave me the mother's name, Sarah Field. Without any corroborating documents I had to turn to DNA to try and prove that Sarah was indeed Caroline's mother.

First, I tracked Sarah Field in the records and found a possible later marriage to William Horton and the birth of a number of children to the couple.

Next, I managed to follow two of the children's descendants down a couple of generations. The children were Samuel and Harriet Horton.

I asked some of my key family members if they would do their DNA tests for me. They were my great uncle Russell Williams (known as Uncle John), my dad and his brothers and my dad's cousin (all Caroline's great, great grandsons). To my great joy they all agreed.

I used a number of DNA matching sites to try and find the matches I needed.

The goal was to find triangulated matches. That is, I needed to find three people who descended from Sarah through different children but who shared exactly the same segment of DNA.

The task was monumental. Each of the DNA tests I was looking at had hundreds of matches and most of these matches had no family tree research associated with them so there was no way to verify which ancestor they shared.

Of the few that had family tree research most shared DNA from different ancestors. The remainder who I surmised were descended from Caroline or Sarah then did not share the same segment of DNA with a third tester. The last requirement for a third matching person ensures the shared segment between two people is not a random match. The third matching person with the same researched ancestor proves that piece of DNA is from that ancestor.

The results were conclusive. I managed to get triangulated matches back to both Sarah and Caroline. One match allowed me to prove that Elizabeth Conroy is Caroline's daughter. There are no paper records linking them.

Permission has been sought to publish the matches' names. Responses for many were not received and their initials are only used.

As a final note I want to thank my relatives for humouring me and letting me test their DNA. The importance of this act has been highlighted with Uncle John's passing. Without his generosity of spirit in allowing me to test his DNA and manage his kit I would not have made these links. Thank you all.

DNA Tester	Chromosome Number	Shared Genomic Segment	Triangulated Matches	MRCA
Russell Williams	4	57090655 – 73676145	CPH, TM, SD	Sarah Field
Russell Williams	4	142839831 – 158854303	PW, LM	Caroline Field
Russell Williams	21	32695264 – 39850639	MH, JT	Caroline Field
John Tarleton	17	68242546 - 72173910	MF, TM, SD	Caroline Field
John Tarleton	3	97939961 – 110697187	CB, SD, JP, RW, RT	Sarah Field
Trevor Corby	2	7240383 – 20236634	MF, LM	Caroline Field
Trevor Corby	9	79146609 – 89279055	DW, NT, RT	Sarah Field

MRCA: Most Recent Common Ancestor

Match	Name	Line of Descent
CB	CB	Sarah Field to Samuel Horton
CPH	Craig Philip Horton	Sarah Field to Samuel Horton
DW	Dawn Woollaston	Sarah Field to Harriett Horton
JP	Jean Priest	Sarah Field to Harriett Horton
JT	John Tarleton	Sarah Field to Caroline Field to John Williams
LM	LM	Sarah Field to Caroline Field to Henry Conroy
MF	MF	Sarah Field to Caroline Field to James Dover
MH	MH	Sarah Field to Caroline Field to Henry Conroy
NT	Neville Tarleton	Sarah Field to Caroline Field to John Williams
PW	PW	Sarah Field to Caroline Field to Henry Conroy
RT	Raymond Tarleton	Sarah Field to Caroline Field to John Williams
RW	Russell Williams	Sarah Field to Caroline Field to John Williams
SD	SD	Sarah Field to Caroline Field to Elizabeth Conroy
TC	Trevor Corby	Sarah Field to Caroline Field to John Williams
TM	TM	Sarah Field to Caroline Field to John Williams

BIBLIOGRAPHY

'1841 England Census for Sarah Horton. Warwickshire, Birmingham, St Paul, District 6. Image 10'. 1841. Ancestry. 1841. https://www.ancestry.com.au.

'1851 England Census for Frederick Horton in West Sheffield, Sheffield, Yorkshire, 15. Image 18.' 1851. Ancestry. Accessed 15 May 2024. https://www.ancestry.com.au.

'1851 England Census, Warwickshire, Birmingham, St Paul, 01.' 1851. Ancestry. Accessed 13 June 2024. https://www.ancestry.com.au.

1861 England Census for Sarah Horton, Warwickshire, Birmingham, St Paul, District 01. Image 16'. 1841. Ancestry. Accessed 13 June 2024. https://www.ancestry.com.au.

'A History of the County of Warwick: Vol 7, the City of Birmingham. Political and Administrative History: Local Government and Public Services.' n.d. British History Online. Accessed 13 June 2024. https://www.british-history.ac.uk/vch/warks/vol7/pp318-353#h3-s4.

A'Beckett, Edward. 1881. *Hamilton Hume F.R.G.S, Explorer*. State Library of Victoria. http://handle.slv.vic.gov.au/10381/303380.

American & Australasian Photographic Company. 1870. *Woman Outside Bark Hut House, Gulgong*. Mitchell Library, State Library of New South Wales. Accessed 28 April 2022. https://collection.sl.nsw.gov.au/record/Yr86Vybn.

Angas, George French. 1851. *Bathurst*. http://handle.slv.vic.gov.au/10381/136967.

Apfel, Lisa. 2023. 'Digital Photograph of 26a. [Shepherd on Bush Property]'. In *Item 02: Sketchbook of Andrew Bonar [1854, ca. 1857-1860, 1913]*. Vol. 2.

Arrowsmith, John. 1838. 'The South Eastern Portion of Australia [Cartographic Material]'. Trove. 1838. National Library of Australia. https://nla.gov.au/nla.obj-230630599.

'Australian Convict Transportation Registers – Other Fleets & Ships, 1791-1868. 1853-1863, Image 151 for Sultana 1859'. n.d. Ancestry. Accessed 13 November 2023. https://www.ancestry.com.au.

'Australian Convict Transportation Registers – Other Fleets & Ships, 1791-1868. 1853-1863, Image 158 for Edwin Horton 1859'. n.d. Ancestry. Accessed 13 November 2023. https://www.ancestry.com.au.

Backler, Joseph. n.d. *[Bathurst], c.1847-57 / Painted by Joseph Backler? (Digitised by Mitchell Library, State Library of New South Wales)*. State Library of New South Wales. Accessed 6 April 2022. https://collection.sl.nsw.gov.au/record/nmQdbvRn/2BNaKJlA8VdbB.

Bathurst Free Press and Mining Journal. 1853. 'Family Notices', 22 January 1853. National Library of Australia. http://nla.gov.au/nla.news-article62047118.

———. 1855. 'Advertising', 7 July 1855. National Library of Australia. http://nla.gov.au/nla.news-article62054300.

Bennett, Michael quoted in *ABC News*. 17 Aug 2018. 'How the Wiradyuri Survived First Contact with European Settlers'. Accessed 2 July 2024. https://www.abc.net.au/news/2018-08-17/curious-central-west-how-the-Wiradyuri-survived-first-contact/10128822.

Birds at Macquarie Marshes (Warren) Western N.S.W. Image 27. 1947. Photograph. Mitchell Library, State Library of New South Wales and Courtesy ACP Magazines Ltd. Accessed 17 April 2022. https://collection.sl.nsw.gov.au/record/Yj7oAdD9.

'Birmingham, England, Church of England Baptisms, 1813-1922 for Caroline Field, Birmingham, St Phillip, 1813-1818. Image 301'. n.d. Ancestry. Accessed 29 March 2022. https://www.ancestry.com.au.

'Birmingham, England, Church of England Baptisms, 1813-1922 for Mary Horton at Bishop Ryder 1849. Image 36'. n.d. Ancestry. Accessed 15 May 2024. https://www.ancestry.com.au.

'Birmingham, England, Church of England Marriages and Banns, 1754-1939 for John Horton at St Philip in 1846. Image 209'. n.d. Ancestry. Accessed 15 May 2024. https://www.ancestry.com.au.

'Birmingham, England, Church of England Marriages and Banns, 1754-1937 for Sarah Field, Aston, St Peter and St Paul, 1817-1820. Image 95'. n.d. Ancestry. Accessed 29 March 2022. https://www.ancestry.com.au.

'Birmingham, England, Church of England Marriages and Banns, 1754-1939 for Harriet Horton, Birmingham, St Martin.' 1849. Ancestry. Accessed 13 June 2024. https://www.ancestry.com.au.

Birmingham Gazette. 5 Nov 1827. 'BIRMINGHAM, Nov. 5, 1827'. British Library Newspapers. Accessed 10 June 2024. 3. https://link.gale.com/apps/doc/EN3216063222/BNCN?sid=bookmark-BNCN&xid=d9312db0.

Birmingham Gazette. 2 Nov 1829. 'BIRMINGHAM, Nov. 2, 1829'. British Library Newspapers. Accessed 3 June 2024. https://link-gale-com.rp.nla.gov.au/apps/doc/EN3216064618/BNCN?sid=bookmark-BNCN&xid=b536ddfe.

Birmingham Gazette. 28 Feb 1842. 'Birmingham Guardians of the Poor.' British Library Newspapers. Accessed 12 June 2024. https://link.gale.com/apps/doc/EN3216072842/BNCN?sid=bookmark-BNCN&xid=de1ce709.

Birmingham Journal. 1831. 'Warwickshire Quarter Sessions', 22 October 1831. https://www.britishnewspaperarchive.co.uk/viewer/BL/0000224/18311022/039/0003?browse=true.

Birmingham Journal. 21 Oct 1843. 'Inquest.' British Newspaper Archive. Accessed 20 June 2024. https://www.britishnewspaperarchive.co.uk/.

Bruce, G. 1831. *Hobart Town Chain Gang*. State Library of New South Wales. https://collection.sl.nsw.gov.au/digital/R5mDqlVXvZVdq.

Captain Charles Sturt [Picture]. 1895. National Library of Australia. Accessed 16 April 2022. https://nla.gov.au/nla.obj-136105796.

'Caroline Field in Calendars of Prisoners, Michaelmas Quarter Session Case 38. Ref. QS 26/2/219'. 1831. Warwickshire Records Office.

'Caroline Hinchley alias Field in Depositions, 1824-1850 in the Warwickshire Quarter Sessions. Film #004414588. Images 255-256'. 1831. FamilySearch. Accessed 2 June 2024. www.familysearch.org.

'Caroline Hinchley in Calendars of Prisoners, 1801-1850, in the Warwickshire Quarter Sessions Film #4415779. Image 340'. 1831. FamilySearch. Accessed 2 June 2024. www.familysearch.org.

Central Board of Health. n.d. *The Cholera Gazette: Consisting of Documents Communicated by the Central Board of Health, with Intelligence Related to the Disease, Derived from Other Authentic Sources Jan 14, 1832.* 2nd ed. Vol. 1. London: S. Highley. Accessed 2 April 2022. https://play.google.com/store/books/details?id=0_EEAAAAQAAJ&rdid=book-0_EEAAAAQAAJ&rdot=1.

Charmichael, John. 1829. *Item 05: Sydney from Woolloomooloo Hill.* Mitchell Library, State Library of New South Wales. Accessed 10 May 2024. https://collection.sl.nsw.gov.au/record/1l4lyNV1/bJAAg6J2pE2Ol.

Coles-Harris, Jenni. n.d. 'A Tour of Lost Birmingham: Street By Street: A Short History of Ann Street.' *A Tour of Lost Birmingham* (blog). Accessed 29 March 2022. https://mappingbirmingham.blogspot.com/2012/01/short-history-of-ann-street.html.

Collection of Views Predominantly of Sydney, Liverpool, and the Sunda Straits, and Portraits, ca 1807, 1829-1847, 1887.(5) Convict Barrack Sydney N.S. Wales. 1820. State Library of New South Wales. https://collection.sl.nsw.gov.au/record/16AJqGqn/4NOW6xjk4kMO0.

'Conduct Registers of Male Convicts Arriving in the Period of the Probation System, CON33-1-6, Lady Raffles, Image 146 Samuel Horton'. n.d. Libraries Tasmania. Accessed 31 October 2023. https://stors.tas.gov.au/CON33-1-6$init=CON33-1-6P146.

'Convict Conduct Record - CON40-1-10 Image 93 Mary Ann Smith'. n.d. Libraries Tasmania. Accessed 10 November 2023. https://stors.tas.gov.au/CON40-1-10$init=CON40-1-10P93.

'Convict Description List CON18-1-26 for Samuel Horton'. n.d. Libraries Tasmania. Accessed 2 November 2023. https://stors.tas.gov.au/CON18-1-26$init=CON18-1-26p127.

'Convict Prisons Bill, Volume 109: Debated on Thursday 14 Mar 1850'. n.d. UK Parliament, Hansard. Accessed 20 May 2024. https://hansard.parliament.uk/Lords/1850-03-14/debates/2d7b9cd4-c746-46dd-80f9-ec23c1ec3445/ConvictPrisonsBill.

[Convict Stockade at Cox's River Crossing near Hartley]. 1831. Mitchell Library, State Library of New South Wales. Accessed 10 May 2024. https://collection.sl.nsw.gov.au/record/1l4l7a51/yxZLXBmdPKMJz.

Cumpston, J.H.L. 1951. *Charles Sturt - His Life and Journeys of Exploration.* Project Gutenberg. https://gutenberg.net.au/ebooks07/0700391h.html#ch3.

Currency Lad. 1833a. 'Shipping Intelligence', 16 February 1833. National Library of Australia. http://nla.gov.au/nla.news-article252637059.

———. 1833b. 'BATHURST.', 16 March 1833. National Library of Australia. http://nla.gov.au/nla.news-article252636401.

'Death Registration: Sarah Horton 1864 Vol 6d p102'. n.d. HM Passport Office. General Register Office. Accessed 9 June 2024. www.gro.gov.uk.

Earle, Augustus. 1826. *Wellington Valley, New South Wales, Looking East from Government House [Picture].* Watercolour. National Library of Australia. https://nla.gov.au/nla.obj-134496732.

———. n.d. *Moolong Plains, near Wellington Valley. N.S.Wales*. Mitchell Library, State Library of New South Wales. Accessed 6 April 2022. https://collection.sl.nsw.gov.au/record/16AJjPon/Gyg5w4mmzML8o.

'England & Wales, Crime, Prisons & Punishments, 1770-1935 for John Horton. Series HO8. Source Home Office: Convict Hulks, Prisons & Criminal Lunatic Asylums: Quarterly Returns of Prisoners. Piece No 118. Page 4'. n.d. Findmypast. Accessed 14 May 2024. https:\\findmypast.com.au.

'England & Wales, Crime, Prisons & Punishments, 1770-1935 for John Horton. Series HO24. Source Millbank Prison Registers: Male Prisoners. Volume 5. Piece No 5'. n.d. Findmypast. Accessed 14 May 2024. https:\\findmypast.com.au.

'England & Wales, Crime, Prisons & Punishments, 1770-1935 for John Horton. Series PCOM2. Source Birmingham Gaol, Warwickshire: Register of Convicts. Piece No 436'. n.d. Findmypast. Accessed 14 May 2024. https:\\findmypast.com.au.

'England & Wales, Criminal Registers, 1791-1892 for Caroline Field. England. Warwickshire. 1831. Image 33'. n.d. Ancestry. Accessed 1 April 2022. https://www.ancestry.com.au.

'England & Wales, Criminal Registers, 1791-1892 for Edwin Horton, Warwickshire. Image 18.' 1857. Ancestry. 1857. https://www.ancestry.com.au.

'England & Wales, Criminal Registers, 1791-1892 for John Horton. England, Worcestershire, Image 5'. 1850. Ancestry. Accessed 16 May 2024. https://www.ancestry.com.au.

'England & Wales, Criminal Registers, 1791-1892 for Samuel Horton, England, Warwickshire. Image 32.' 1840. Ancestry. 1840. https://www.ancestry.com.au.

Evans, William. 1821. 'Royal Navy Medical Journals, 1817-1856. H. Hindostan. 25 Jun 1821-29 Nov 1821. Image 8'. Ancestry. 1821. https://www.ancestry.com.au.

Frith, William Powell. 1880. *1962P1 Retribution*. Birmingham Museums Trust. Accessed 31 May 2024. https://dams.birminghammuseums.org.uk/asset-bank/action/viewAsset?id=6755&index=2&total=4&view=viewSearchItem

Frost, Lucy. 2006. 'Female Factories'. The Companion to Tasmanian History. 2006. https://www.utas.edu.au/library/companion_to_tasmanian_history/F/Female%20factories.htm.

Geelong Advertiser. 1849. 'GEELONG MARKETS.', 14 April 1849. National Library of Australia. http://nla.gov.au/nla.news-article93139106.

GeniCert, trans. 2021. 'Transcript of New South Wales Death Certificate #1902/7447 for James Dover'.

———, trans. 2021. 'Transcript of New South Wales Marriage Certificate #1860/2278 for James Dover and Eliza Dunn'.

———, trans. 2022. 'Transcript of New South Wales Death Certificate #1915/16610 for Samuel Dover'.

———, trans. 2022. 'Transcript of New South Wales Death Certificate #1856/2706 for George Conroy'.

———, trans. 2022. 'Transcript of New South Wales Death Certificate

#1925/8040 for Elizabeth Dunn'.
———, trans. 2022. 'Transcript of New South Wales Marriage Certificate #1869/3091 for John Dunne and Elizabeth Conroy'.
———, trans. 2023. 'Transcript of New South Wales Death Certificate #1935/6966 for Henry Conroy'.
———, trans. 2023. 'Transcript of New South Wales Marriage Certificate #1874/3466 for William House and Caroline Conroy'.
———, trans. 2023. 'Transcript of New South Wales Marriage Certificate #1881/4701 for Henry Cornroy (Sic) and Malvina Jane Johnson'.
Gennys, R. H. 1925. 'Shepherds and Shepherding in Australia.' *The Royal Australian Historical Society*, Part 5, 11: 281–88. National Library of Australia. https://nla.gov.au/nla.obj-594390116.
Gill, John Thomas Doyle & Samuel Thomas. n.d. *Dr Doyle's Sketch Book. F9 Prospecting at an out Station. Dingoes, or Wild Dogs of the Bush Prowling Round the Sheep Fold*. State Library of New South Wales. Accessed 7 May 2022. https://digital.sl.nsw.gov.au/delivery/DeliveryManagerServlet?embedded=true&toolbar=false&dps_pid=IE1002343&_ga=2.136071734.640366620.1651659857-1116325754.1619962950.
Gill, Samuel Thomas. 1849. *Shepherd, So. [i.e. South] Australia, Adelaide, Jany 1849*. National Library of Australia. Accessed 5 May 2022. https://nla.gov.au/nla.obj-134370033.
———.1855. *Out Sheep Station*. National Library of Australia. Accessed 5 May 2022. https://nla.gov.au/nla.obj-2821263488.
———. n.d. 'F9 Prospecting at an out Station. Dingoes, or Wild Dogs of the Bush Prowling Round the Sheep Fold.' In *Dr Doyle's Sketch Book*. Accessed 7 May 2022. https://collection.sl.nsw.gov.au/record/nQR2plX1.
———. n.d. *Samuel Thomas Gill Original Sketches, 1844-1866. 38. [The Stockman]*. Mitchell Library, State Library of New South Wales. Accessed 12 April 2022. https://collection.sl.nsw.gov.au/digital/eDwQ0yj7oK4b.
Gooderson, Philip. 2010. *The Gangs of Birmingham*. Milo Books Ltd. Google-Books-ID:HOFmDwAAQBAJ
Govett, William Romaine. n.d. 'Incident on the Road at Victoria Pass between Pp 6-7 of William Govett Notes and Sketches Taken during a Surveying Expedition in N. South Wales and Blue Mountains Road by William Govett on Staff of Major Mitchell, Surveyor General of New South Wales, 1830-1835.' State Library
Grant, Andrew. 2010. 'Powerhouse Collection - Reading Type Horse-Drawn Caravan'. Powerhouse Collection. 2010. https://collection.powerhouse.com.au/object/408922.
'Gudyarra (War/Battle with Spears)'. 2024. Dhuluny. Accessed 3 July 2024. https://www.dhuluny.com.au/gudyarra-war-battle-with-spears.
Hacker, Edward H. n.d. *The New Sporting Magazine Vol 14 January 1838. No. 81*. Google. Accessed 4 April 2024. https://play.google.com/store/books/details?id=wvM7AAAAIAAJ.
Hampshire/Portsmouth Telegraph. 31 Dec 1853. 'FREE TRADE PROGRESS.' British Library Newspapers. Accessed 20 May 2024.

https://link.gale.com/apps/doc/BB3206055511/BNCN?sid=bookmark-BNCN&xid=d4f11cde.
Harman, Thomas T. n.d. 'Showell's Dictionary of Birmingham.' Project Gutenberg. Accessed 09 April 2024. https://www.gutenberg.org/ebooks/14472.
Hendy-Pooley, Grace. 1905. 'Early History of Bathurst and Surroundings'. *Journal and Proceedings The Australian Historical Society*, 28 November 1905. https://www.rahs.org.au/wp-content/uploads/2015/05/08_Reflecting_Early-History-of-Bathurst-and-Surroundings.pdf.
'Historical Australian Towns: Bathurst, NSW: Australia's First Inland Settlement.' n.d. *Historical Australian Towns* (blog). Accessed 5 April 2022. https://historicalaustraliantowns.blogspot.com/2018/02/bathurst-australias-first-inland.html.
Horse Drawn Prison van or 'Black Maria.' 1907. Queensland Police Museum. https://ehive.com/collections/3606/objects/553902/horse-drawn-prison-van-or-black-maria.
Howarth, Jennifer. 2023. 'A History of the Burials in Lewis Ponds Cemetery 1861-1919'. *Submitted in Partial Fulfilment of the Diploma of Family Historical Studies of the Society of Australian Genealogists*.
Hutton, William. 1836. *An History of Birmingham*. 6th ed. Birmingham, England: James Guest. Accessed 13 May 2024. http://archive.org/details/historybirmingh00huttgoog.
Illustrated Sydney News. 1872. 'Sheep Hurdles', 20 February 1872. National Library of Australia. http://nla.gov.au/nla.news-article63618536.
'Indents of Male Convicts CON14-1-8 for Samuel Horton, Images 34-35'. n.d. Libraries Tasmania. Accessed 1 November 2023. https://stors.tas.gov.au/CON14-1-8$init=CON14-1-8P34.
Inquirer. 12 Apr 1854. 'SHIPPING INTELLIGENCE.' Accessed 20 May 2024. http://nla.gov.au/nla.news-article65741021.
Inquirer and Commercial News. 1 Aug 1855. 'The Inquirer & Commercial News. WEDNESDAY, AUGUST 1, 1855.' Accessed 23 May 2024. http://nla.gov.au/nla.news-article66007141.
Inquirer and Commercial News. 19 Sep 1855. 'PUBLIC MEETING AT PERTH.' Accessed 23 May 2024. http://nla.gov.au/nla.news-article66006651.
Inquirer and Commercial News. 26 Sep 1855. 'The Inquirer & Commercial News. Quid Verum at Que Decens, Curo et Rogo, et Omnis in Hoc Sum WEDNESDAY, SEPTEMBER 26, 1855.' Accessed 21 May 2024. http://nla.gov.au/nla.news-article66006584.
Jebb, Joshua. 1844. *Report of the Surveyor-General of Prisons on the Construction, Ventilation, and Details of Pentonville Prison.* London: Printed by W. Clowes and sons for H.M. Stationery Office. Accessed 13 November 2023. 5. http://archive.org/details/b29300915.
Leamington Spa Courier. 7 Feb 1829. 'Warwick.' British Library Newspapers. Accessed 3 June 2024. https://link-gale-com.rp.nla.gov.au/apps/doc/JA3230983899/BNCN?sid=bookmark-BNCN&xid=81bd9cf1.
Logan, Francis. n.d. 'UK, Royal Navy Medical Journals, 1817-1856. Fanny. 02

Jun 1832-19 Feb 1833'. Ancestry. Accessed 2 April 2022. https://www.ancestry.com.au/

Mackie, Frederick. 1853. *The Cap Worn by the Separate Treatment Prisoners.* Accessed 10 May 2024. https://nla.gov.au/nla.obj-138954202.

'Main Series of Letters Received,1826-1982. [4-2201-2] 33_2396. Evernden to Colonial Secretary.' 1833, 1833. Museums of History NSW - State Archives Collection.

'Marriage Permission for Samuel Horton and Margaret Smedley.' 1848. Item. Libraries Tasmania. https://stors.tas.gov.au/CON52-1-2p200j2k.

'Marriage Registration Samuel Horton and Margaret Smedley.' 1848. Item. Libraries Tasmania. https://stors.tas.gov.au/NI/837117.

Maxwell, John. 1982. *Letters of John Maxwell, Superintendent of Government Stock, 1823-31.* Wangaratta, Victoria: Shoestring Press.

Middleton, Alex, and Francis Beresford Maning. 1886. *Bathurst and Western District Directory and Tourist's Guide and Gazetteer*. Bathurst: J. Virtue & Company.

Mitchell, Thomas. 1830. 'Opp. P8 Sketch of Roads to Bathurst in: Illustrations from Progress in Public Works & Roads in NSW, 1827-1855. Image 7'. State Library of New South Wales. Accessed 6 April 2022. https://collection.sl.nsw.gov.au/record/92eVDzPY/265w7QO20MEX0r.

Mitchell, Thomas. 1833. *Plan for the Town of Bathurst.* National Library of Australia. Accessed 6 April 2022. http://nla.gov.au/nla.obj-1494744991.

Morning Chronicle (1801). 27 Dec 1853. 'EVENING EDITION.' British Library Newspapers. Accessed 20 May 2024. https://link.gale.com/apps/doc/Y3207231311/BNCN?sid=bookmark-BNCN&xid=1794b534.

Morning Post. 1850. 'Multiple News Items', 13 March 1850. British Library Newspapers. https://link.gale.com/apps/doc/R3211631380/BNCN?sid=bookmark-BNCN&xid=8e208332.

Murrin, Joy, trans. 2009. 'Transcript of New South Wales Death Certificate #1917/15873 for William Williams'.

———, trans. 2009. 'Transcript of New South Wales Marriage Certificate #1871/3116 for William Williams and Sarah Ann Smalley'.

Nejedly, Mary. n.d. 'Child Labour in an Industrial Town: A Study of Child Workers in Birmingham, 1750 to 1880. July 2018'. UBira E Theses. University of Birmingham. Accessed 29 March 2022. https://etheses.bham.ac.uk/id/eprint/9026/1/Nejedly2019PhD.pdf.

'New South Wales, Australia, Colonial Secretary's Papers, 1788-1856. Special Bundles, 1794-1825. Image 2943.' 1822. Ancestry. 1822. https://www.ancestry.com.au.

'New South Wales, Australia, Colonial Secretary's Papers, 1788-1856, Special Bundles, 1794-1825. Image 2946'. 1823. 1823. https://www.ancestry.com.au.

'New South Wales, Australia, Colonial Secretary's Papers, 1788-1856. Special Bundles, 1794-1825. Image 6198.' 1821. Ancestry. 1821. https://www.ancestry.com.au.

'New South Wales, Australia, Colonial Secretary's Papers. Main Series of Letters Received, 1788-1826. Depositions of John Softly and John Epstien.

Image 25217'. 1824. Ancestry. Accessed 13 April 2022. https://www.ancestry.com.au.
'New South Wales, Australia, Colonial Secretary's Papers. Main Series of Letters Received, 1788-1826. Maxwell to Goulburn. Image 24935'. 1823. Ancestry. Accessed 13 April 2022. https://www.ancestry.com.au.
'New South Wales, Australia, Colonial Secretary's Papers. Main Series of Letters Received, 1788-1826. Morrisett to Goulburn. Image 25230'. 1824. Ancestry. 1824. https://www.ancestry.com.au.
'New South Wales, Australia, Settler and Convict Lists, 1787-1834. Convicts Arrived 1833-1834. Image 253'. n.d. Ancestry. Accessed 3 April 2022. https://www.ancestry.com.au.
'New South Wales, Australia, Tickets of Leave, 1810-1869 for James Dauber. (NRS12202), May1829-Dec 1829. Image 227'. n.d. Ancestry. Accessed 7 April 2022. https://www.ancestry.com.au.
'New South Wales, Australia, Tickets of Leave, 1810-1869 for James Norman. (NRS 12202), May1829-Dec 1829. Image 224'. n.d. Ancestry. Accessed 16 April 2022. https://www.ancestry.com.au.
'New South Wales, Australia, Tickets of Leave, 1810-1869 for James Smith. (NRS 12202), May1829-Dec 1829. Image 230'. n.d. Ancestry. Accessed 16 April 2022. https://www.ancestry.com.au.
'New South Wales, Australia, Tickets of Leave, 1810-1869 for John Williams. (NRS 12202), May1829-Dec 1829. Image 231'. n.d. Ancestry. Accessed 16 April 2022. https://www.ancestry.com.au.
'New South Wales, Australia, Tickets of Leave, 1810-1869 for Owen Reilly. ((NRS 12202), May 1829-Dec 1829, Image 416'. n.d. Ancestry. Accessed 15 August 2023. https://www.ancestry.com.au.
'New South Wales, Australia, Tickets of Leave, 1810-1869 for Owen Reilly. (NRS 12202), May1829-Dec 1829. Image 229'. n.d. Ancestry. Accessed 16 April 2022. https://www.ancestry.com.au.
'New South Wales, Australia, Tickets of Leave, 1810-1869 for Peter Snow. (NRS 12202), May1829-Dec 1829. Image 225'. n.d. Ancestry. Accessed 16 April 2022. https://www.ancestry.com.au.
'New South Wales, Australia, Tickets of Leave, 1810-1869, for Samuel Henwood. (NRS 12202), May1829-Dec 1829. Image 223'. n.d. Ancestry. Accessed 16 April 2022. https://www.ancestry.com.au.
'New South Wales, Australia, Tickets of Leave, 1810-1869 for Stephen Peck. (NRS 12202), May1829-Dec 1829. Image 228'. n.d. Ancestry. Accessed 16 April 2022. https://www.ancestry.com.au.
'New South Wales, Australia, Tickets of Leave, 1810-1869 for William Bryant. (NRS 12202), May1829-Dec 1829. Image 226'. n.d. Ancestry. Accessed 16 April 2022. https://www.ancestry.com.au.
New South Wales Births, Deaths and Marriages. 2019. 'Death Certificate #3086/1903 for John Williams'.
'New South Wales, Census and Population Books, Wellington Valley Population Book. Image 8.' 1825. Ancestry. 1825. https://www.ancestry.com.au.
New South Wales Government Gazette. 1837. 'PARDONS.', 1 November 1837. National Library of Australia. http://nla.gov.au/nla.news-article230670940.
———. 1839. 'Government Gazette Notices', 20 February 1839. National Library

of Australia. http://nla.gov.au/nla.news-article230382935.
North Devon Journal. 13 Jun 1850. 'County Intelligence.' British Library Newspapers. Accessed 20 May 2024. https://link.gale.com/apps/doc/IG3225161276/BNCN?sid=bookmark-BNCN&xid=32517863.
North Western Advocate and the Emu Bay Times. 1900. 'BLACK RIVER.', 10 May 1900. National Library of Australia. http://nla.gov.au/nla.news-article64491343.
'Nowland's Mail Coach.' n.d. National Museum of Australia. Accessed 13 August 2023. https://www.nma.gov.au/explore/collection/highlights/nowlands-mail-coach.
NSW Land Registry Services. 2023. 'County: Bathurst, Parish: Bathurst, Sheet 1, Edition 6'. Historical Lands Records Viewer. 2023. https://hlrv.nswlrs.com.au/.
Nuttall, Bryan. 2014. 'Birmingham's Manufacturing History'. *RH Nuttall* (blog). 11 February 2014. https://www.rhnuttall.co.uk/blog/birminghams-manufacturing-history/.
'Park Street Burial Ground and Birmingham's Population Expansion.' n.d. *MOLA Headland Infrastructure* (blog). Accessed 1 June 2024. https://molaheadland.com/park-street-burial-ground-and-birminghams-population-expansion/.
'Pentonville Prison.' n.d. 19th Century Prison History. Accessed 13 November 2023. https://www.prisonhistory.org/prison/pentonville-prison-2/.
'Permission To Marry.' 2022. Female Convicts Research Centre Inc. 10 April 2022. https://www.femaleconvicts.org.au/administration/ptom.
Perth DPS. n.d. 'Physical Descriptions of Convicts on the Sea Park, 1854'. Convicts to Australia. Accessed 25 May 2024. https://www.perthdps.com/.
Perth Gazette and Independent Journal of Politics and News. 21 Apr 1854. 'Domestic Sayings and Doings.' Accessed 20 May 2024. http://nla.gov.au/nla.news-article3175162.
Perth Gazette and Independent Journal of Politics and News. 21 Sep 1855. 'THE INDEPENDENT JOURNAL.' Accessed 23 May 2024. http://nla.gov.au/nla.news-article3176417.
Perth Gazette and Independent Journal of Politics and News. 23 Aug 1861. 'Perth Police Court.,' 23 August 1861. National Library of Australia. http://nla.gov.au/nla.news-article2933346.
'Physical Descriptions of Convicts on the Sultana, 1859'. n.d. Convicts to Australia. https://www.perthdps.com/convicts/conwad26.htm.
Pickard, John. 2008. 'Shepherding in Colonial Australia'. *Rural History* 19 (1): 55–80. https://doi.org/10.1017/S0956793307002300.
'Registers of Applications for Permission to Marry, CON52/1/2 Page 379 for Samuel Horton and Mary Ann Smith'. 1847. Item. Libraries Tasmania. https://libraries.tas.gov.au/Record/NamesIndex/1254190.
'Registers of Baptisms, Burials and Marriages, Series NRS 12937, Reel 5005, Baptism James Dober, V18371504 22'. 1837. Museums of History NSW - State Archives Collection.
'Registers of Baptisms, Burials and Marriages, Series NRS 12937, Reel 5006,

Burial James Donner V1841282 25B'. 1841. Museums of History NSW - State Archives Collection.
'Registers of Baptisms, Burials and Marriages, Series NRS 12937, Reel 5009, Baptism John W Williams, V18411933 31A'. 1841. Museums of History NSW - State Archives Collection.
'Registers of Baptisms, Burials and Marriages, Series NRS 12937, Reel 5009, Baptism Sarah Williams, V18441934 31A'. 1844. Museums of History NSW - State Archives Collection.
'Registers of Baptisms, Burials and Marriages, Series NRS 12937, Reel 5026, Baptism Caroline Conroy, V1852822 70'. 1841. Museums of History NSW - State Archives Collection.
'Registry Records.' n.d. NSW Registry of Births Deaths & Marriages. NSW Government. Accessed 13 October 2023. https://www.nsw.gov.au/family-and-relationships/family-history-search/registry-records.
Roberts, David Andrew. 2000. 'A Sort of Inland Norfolk Island: Isolation, Coercion and Resistance on the Wellington Valley Convict Station, 1823-26'. *Journal of Australian Colonial History* 2 (1): 50–73. https://doi.org/10.3316/ielapa.200011056.
———. 2006. '"The Valley of Swells" "Special" or "Educated" Convicts on the Wellington Valley Settlement, 1827–1830'. *History Australia* 3 (1): 11.1-11.21. https://doi.org/10.2104/ha060011.
'"Royal Tar" Wooden Barque at Port Adelaide.' n.d. State Library of South Australia. Accessed 3 April 2022. https://collections.slsa.sa.gov.au/resource/PRG+1373/42/14.
'Samuel Horton in Calendars of Prisoners, 1801-1850, in the Warwickshire Quarter Sessions Film #4415779. Image 490'. 1837. FamilySearch. Accessed 2 June 2024. www.familysearch.org
'Samuel Horton in Depositions, 1824-1850 in the Warwickshire Quarter Sessions. Film #004415095. Images 401-402'. 1837. FamilySearch. Accessed 2 June 2024. www.familysearch.org
Sea Park, Journal of Joseph Caldwell, Surgeon, December 1853- April 1854 (File (TNA: Adm 101/253/1E)). AJCP Digitised Copy.' n.d. National Library of Australia. Accessed 20 May 2024. https://nla.gov.au/nla.obj-2702880146.
Sketch on the Bogan River. 1870. State Library of Victoria. Accessed 3 May 2024. http://handle.slv.vic.gov.au/10381/252354
Smith, William (Topographer). 1830. *A New & Compendious History, of the County of Warwick*. Birmingham, W. Emans. Accessed 2 June 2024. 31. http://archive.org/details/newcompendioushi01smit.
South Australian Gazette and Mining Journal. 1849. 'LIFE IN THE BUSH — THE SHEPHERD.', 17 February 1849. National Library of Australia. http://nla.gov.au/nla.news-article195937150.
Southey, Thomas. 1848. *The Rise, Progress and Present State of Colonial Wools : With Some Account of the Goat's Wool and Angora and India*. Smith, Elder.
Sprod, Michael. 2006. 'Probation System'. The Companion to Tasmanian History-Probation System. 2006. https://www.utas.edu.au/library/companion_to_tasmanian_history/P/Pro

bation%20system.htm.
Stock, Edward. 1850. *Sheep Station on the Lachlan River, (Messers Philps & Chadwick)*. Drawing. Accessed 1 May 2022. http://handle.slv.vic.gov.au/10381/56769.
Sturt, Charles. 1829. 'Government Order'. *Sydney Gazette and New South Wales Advertiser*, 5 May 1829. National Library of Australia. http://nla.gov.au/nla.news-article2192371.
———. 2004. *Two Expeditions into the Interior of Southern Australia*. Project Gutenberg. https://www.gutenberg.org/files/4330/4330-h/4330-h.htm#ap1.1.
Sydney Gazette and New South Wales Advertiser. 19 Aug 1824. 'NEW SOUTH WALES.' Accessed 4 July 2024.1. http://nla.gov.au/nla.news-article2183147.
———.1824. 'Extracts from the Latest London Journals.', 14 October 1824. National Library of Australia. http://nla.gov.au/nla.news-article2183282.
———.14 Oct 1824. 'SUPREME COURT, SATURDAY, OCT. 10.' Accessed 3 July 2024. 2. http://nla.gov.au/nla.news-article2183288.
———. 1825. 'PRINCIPAL SUPERINTENDRNT'S OFFICE. SYDNEY, JANUARY 25, 1825.', 27 January 1825. National Library of Australia. http://nla.gov.au/nla.news-article2183659.
———. 19 Jan 1832. 'AN EXCURSION FROM BATHURST TO WELLINGTON VALLEY.' National Library of Australia. Accessed 5 July 2024. http://nla.gov.au/nla.news-article2204528.
———. 1833. 'Agricultural Report for February 1833. Nepean,' 7 March 1833. National Library of Australia. http://nla.gov.au/nla.news-article2211045.
———. 1835. 'EXTRAORDINARY PROSECUTION.', 1 August 1835. National Library of Australia. http://nla.gov.au/nla.news-article2199505.
Sydney Herald. 1833. 'Shipping Intelligence. Arrivals,' 4 February 1833. National Library of Australia. http://nla.gov.au/nla.news-article12846196.
———. 1840. 'LACHLAN RIVER.', 16 October 1840. National Library of Australia. http://nla.gov.au/nla.news-article12866064.
Sydney Monitor. 1837. 'SCANDALOUS OUTRAGE.', 8 May 1837. National Library of Australia. http://nla.gov.au/nla.news-article32155912.
Sydney Monitor (NSW:1828-1838). 1837. 'Bathurst.', 31 July 1837. National Library of Australia. http://nla.gov.au/nla.news-article32156820.
The Carlisle Kid. n.d. 'Former Cell Door - Barrack Street, Warwick-April 2019'. Geograph. Accessed 9 April 2024. https://www.geograph.org.uk/photo/6117556.
The Australian. 1845. 'To the Editor of the Australian.', 23 October 1845. National Library of Australia. http://nla.gov.au/nla.news-article37155747.
The Illustrated London News. 1843. 'The Pentonville Prison', 7 January 1843. The Illustrated London News Historical Archive, 1842-2003. https://link.gale.com/apps/doc/HN3100005957/ILN?sid=bookmark-ILN&xid=99d37a9f.
'The King v Caroline Field in Depositions, 1824-1850 in the Warwickshire Quarter Sessions. Film #004414588. Images 37-40'. 1831. FamilySearch. Accessed 2 June 2024.

https://www.familysearch.org/search/catalog/show?availability=Family%20History%20Library
'The Parliamentary Report on Transportation (1838)'. 2002. Extracts from the Molesworth Report of 1838. The Victorian Web. Accessed 20 May 2024. https://victorianweb.org/history/transpor.html.
The Standard. 3 Jan 1854. 'Multiple News Items.' British Library Newspapers. Accessed 20 May 2024. https://link.gale.com/apps/doc/R3212197548/BNCN?sid=bookmark-BNCN&xid=5c242e0b.
'The Wellington Valley Project. Letters and Journals Relating to the Church Missionary Society Mission to Wellington Valley, NSW, 1830-45. A Critical Electronic Edition.' 2002. The University of Newcastle, Australia. 2002. https://downloads.newcastle.edu.au/library/cultural%20collections/the-wellington-valley-project/.
The Western Australian Government Gazette. 14 Aug 1855. 'Conditional Pardons.' Western Australian Legislation Website. Accessed 23 May 2024. https://www.legislation.wa.gov.au/legislation/statutes.nsf/gazettes.html
The Western Australian Government Gazette. 16 Jul 1861. 'Ticket of Leave Holders Sentence Expired.' Western Australian Legislation Website. Accessed 23 May 2024. https://www.legislation.wa.gov.au/legislation/statutes.nsf/gazettes.html.
'Transportation Register of Convicts Bound for New South Wales on the Convict Ship Fanny. Caroline Field HO 11/8/370'. 1832. The National Archives, Kew.
Turtle, Laurence, trans. 2008. 'Transcript of New South Wales Marriage Certificate #1878/4326 for John Williams and Sarah Fardell'.
———, trans. 2008. 'Transcript of New South Wales Marriage Certificate #1860/2273 for John Williams and Sophia Jane Manning'.
'UK, Criminal Records, 1780-1871 for Edwin Horton, Prison Registers and Statistical Returns, 1856-1857, HO 24/7, Image 221'. n.d. Ancestry. Accessed 11 November 2023. https://www.ancestry.com.au.
'UK, Prison Hulk Registers and Letter Books, 1802-1849 for Samuel Horton. Fortitude Register 1837-1843, Image 102'. 1840. Ancestry. 1840. https://www.ancestry.com.au.
'Warwick Prison, Cape Road.' n.d. *Our Warwickshire* (blog). Accessed 1 April 2022. https://www.ourwarwickshire.org.uk/content/article/warwick-prison-cape-road.
'Warwickshire Baptisms. St Martin's, Birmingham for Harriet Horton. Baptised 27 May 1831'. Findmypast. Accessed 31 March 2022. www.findmypast.com.au.
'Warwickshire Baptisms. St Martin's, Birmingham for John and Alfred Horton. Baptised 1 Sep 1828'. Findmypast. Accessed 31 March 2022. www.findmypast.com.au.
'Warwickshire Baptisms. St Martin in Birmingham for Joseph and Samuel Horton. Baptised 2 Sep 1822'. Findmypast. Accessed 31 March 2022. https://www.findmypast.com.au/.
Watson, W.L., and Col. Mundy. 1852. *Fording the Bell River [Picture] / on*

Stone by W.L. Walton, from a Sketch by Col. Mundy. 1 print : lithograph ; 11 x 18.2 cm. National Library of Australia.
'Western Australia, Australia, Convict Records, 1846-1930, Convict Department, Registers (128/38-39), Image 163 for Edward Horton'. n.d. Ancestry. Accessed 14 November 2023. https://www.ancestry.com.au.
'Western Australia, Australia, Convict Records, 1846-1930, Convict Department Registers, General Register, 1850-1868 (R21b), Image 398 for Edward Horton'. n.d. Ancestry. Accessed 14 November 2023. https://www.ancestry.com.au.
Western Australia Convict department. 1975. '2905 John Horton. Image 107.' In *General Register of Convicts, 1848-1900 Microfilmed by the Genealogical Society of Salt Lake City. Film 918764*. Salt Lake City. Accessed 23 May 2024.
Westmorland Gazette. 1821. 'Lancaster Assizes', 7 April 1821. British Newspaper Archive. https://www.britishnewspaperarchive.co.uk/viewer/bl/0000399/18210407/009/0003.
Wiblin, Sue. 2019. 'Female Convicts at Bathurst, 1820-1840: A Preliminary Study of Demography, Management and Marriage in Colonial New South Wales'. *Journal of Australian Colonial History* 21: 25–68. https://search-informit-org.ezproxy.slv.vic.gov.au/doi/10.3316/ielapa.856321164464022.
'Wills, AD961-1-8 Will Number 2137 for Samuel Horton'. 1900. Item. Libraries Tasmania. https://libraries.tas.gov.au/Record/NamesIndex/1725052.

INDEX

A

B

C

D

F

G

H

J

K

L

M

N

O

P

R

S

T

W

Y

Milton Keynes UK
Ingram Content Group UK Ltd.
UKHW020058120824
446659UK00007B/26